# Integrated Strategic Change

## How OD Builds Competitive Advantage

# Integrated Strategic Change

## How OD Builds Competitive Advantage

**Christopher G. Worley**
*Pepperdine University*

**David E. Hitchin**
*Pepperdine University*

**Walter L. Ross**
*Covey Leadership Center*

▲▼▼

**ADDISON-WESLEY PUBLISHING COMPANY**
*Reading, Massachusetts • Menlo Park, California • New York*
*Don Mills, Ontario • Wokingham, England • Amsterdam • Bonn*
*Sydney • Singapore • Tokyo • Madrid • San Juan • Milan • Paris*

**Library of Congress Cataloging-in-Publication Data**

HD
58.8
.W684
1996

Worley, Christopher G.
    Integrated strategic change : how OD builds competitive advantage
    / Christopher G. Worley, David E. Hitchin, Walter L. Ross.
        p. cm. - - (Addison-Wesley series on organizational development)
    Includes bibliographical references.
    ISBN 0-201-85777-4 (pbk.)
    1. Organizational change- -Management.  2. Strategic planning.
3. Competition.  I. Hitchin, David.  II. Ross, Walter L. (Walter
Lee), 1940–  .  III. Title.  IV. Series.
HD58.8.W684  21995
658.4'012--dc20                                                                  95-22217
                                                                                              CIP

This book is in the Addison-Wesley Series on Organizational Development.
Editors: Edgar H. Schein, Richard Beckhard

Reprinted with corrections October, 1996

ISBN 0-201-85777-4
    4 5 6 7 8 9 10-BA-989796

# Other Titles in the Organization Development Series

*Organizational Learning: II Theory, Method, and Practice*
Chris Argyris and Donald A. Schön
1996 (62983)
This text addresses how business firms, governments, non-governmental organizations, schools, health care systems, regions, and whole nations need to adapt to changing environments, draw lessons from past successes and failures, detect and correct the errors of the past, anticipate and respond to impending threats, conduct experiments, engage in continuing innovation, and build and realize images of a desirable future. There is a virtual consensus that we are all subject to a "learning imperative," and in the academy no less than in the world of practice, organizational learning has become an idea in good currency.

*Team Building: Current Issues and New Alternatives, Third Edition*
William G. Dyer
1995 (62882)
One of the major developments in the field of organization redesign has been the emergence of self-directed work teams. This book explains how teams are most successful when the team becomes part of the culture and structure or systems of the organization. It discusses the major new trends and emphasizes the degree of commitment that managers and members must bring to the team-building process. It is written for managers and human resource professionals who want to develop a more systematic program of team building in their organization or work unit.

*Creating Labor-Management Partnerships*
Warner P. Woodworth and Christopher B. Meek
1995 (58823)
This book begins with a call for changing the social and political barriers existing in unionized work settings and emphasizes the critical need for union-management cooperation in the present context of international competition. It demonstrates the shift from confrontational union-management relationships toward more effective and positive systems of collaboration. It is written for human resource management and industrial relations managers and staff, union officials, professional arbitrators and mediators, government officials, and professors and students involved in the study of organization development.

*Organization Development: A Process of Learning and Changing,*
*Second Edition*
W. Warner Burke
1994 (50835)
This text presents an overview of OD and looks at OD in part as a change of an organization's culture. It looks at the organization and factors that will influence structure and development in the future. The author also introduces new topics such as information management and strategy implementation.

*Competing with Flexible Lateral Organizations, Second Edition*
Jay R. Galbraith
1994 (50836)
This book focuses on creating competitive advantage by building a lateral capability, enabling a firm to respond flexibly in an uncertain world. The book addresses international coordination and cross business coordination as well as the usual cross functional efforts. It is unique in covering both cross functional (lateral or horizontal) coordination, as well as international and corporate issues.

*The Dynamics of Organizational Levels:*
*A Change Framework for Managers and Consultants*
Nicholas S. Rashford and David Coghlan
1994 (54323)
This book introduces the idea that, for successful change to occur, organizational interventions have to be coordinated across the major levels of issues that all organizations face. Individual level, team level, inter-unit level, and organizational level issues are identified and analyzed, and the kinds of intervention appropriate to each level are spelled out.

*Total Quality: A User's Guide for Implementation*
Dan Ciampa
1992 (54992)
This is a book that directly addresses the challenge of how to make Total Quality work in a practical, no-nonsense way. The companies that will dominate markets in the future will be those that deliver high quality, competitively priced products and service just when the customer wants them and in a way that exceeds the customer's expectations. The vehicle by which these companies move to that stage is Total Quality.

*Parallel Learning Structures: Increasing Information in Bureaucracies*
Gervase R. Bushe and A. B. Shani
1991 (52427)
Parallel learning structures are technostructural interventions that promote system-wide change in bureaucracies while retaining the advantages of bureaucratic design. This text serves as a resource of models and theories built around five cases

of parallel learning structures that can help those who create and maintain them be more effective and successful. For those new to parallel learning structures, the text provides practical advice as to when and how to use them.

## *Managing in the New Team Environment: Skills, Tools, and Methods*
Larry Hirschhorn

1991 (52503)

This text is designed to help manage the tensions and complexities that arise for managers seeking to guide employees in a team environment. Based on an interactive video course developed at IBM, the text takes managers step by step through the process of building a team and authorizing it to act while they learn to step back and delegate. Specific issues addressed are how to give a team structure, how to facilitate its basic proccesses, and how to acknowledge differences in relationships among team members and between the manager and individual team members.

## *Leading Business Teams: How Teams Can Use Technology and Group Process Tools to Enhance Performance*
Robert Johansen, David Sibbett, Suzyn Benson, Alexia Martin,
Robert Mittman, and Paul Saffo

1991 (52829)

What technology or tools should organization development people or team leaders have at their command, now and in the future? This text explores the intersection of technology and business teams, a new and largely uncharted area that goes by several labels, including "groupware," a term that encompasses both electronic and nonelectronic tools for teams. This is the first book of its kind from the field describing what works for business teams and what does not.

## *Becoming a Learning Organization: Beyond the Learning Curve*
Joop Sweiringa and André Wierdsma

1991 (62753)

As organizations evolve with time, the ability to learn and change is becoming increasingly more important. The future poses numerous obstacles and challenges for all organizations, and having the proper learning tools will provide a necessary competitive advantage. This text not only analyzes what a learning organization is, it also explores practical approaches and tools that teach a company to "learn to learn." The aim of this book is to identify and define the learning process, but also to begin the implementation of it in order to gain an advantage in a highly competitive environment.

## *The Conflict-Positive Organization: Stimulate Diversity and Create Unity*
Dean Tjosvold

1991 (51485)

This book describes how managers and employees can use conflict to find common ground, solve problems, and strengthen morale and relationships. By showing how well-managed conflict invigorates and empowers teams and organizations, the text demonstrates how conflict is vital for a company's continuous improvement and increased competitive advantage.

### Change by Design
Robert R. Blake, Jane Srygley Mouton, and Anne Adams McCanse
1989 (50748)
This book develops a systematic approach to organization development and provides readers with rich illustrations of coherent planned change. The book involves testing, examining, revising, and strengthening conceptual foundations in order to create sharper corporate focus and increased predictability of successful organization development.

### Organization Development in Health Care
R. Wayne Boss
1989 (18364)
This is the first book to discuss the intricacies of the health care industry. The book explains the impact of OD in creating healthy and viable organizations in the health care sector. Through unique and innovative techniques, hospitals are able to reduce nursing turnover, thereby resolving the nursing shortage problem. The text also addresses how OD can improve such bottom-line variables as cash flow and net profits.

### Self-Designing Organizations:
### Learning How to Create High Performance
Susan Albers Mohrman and Thomas G. Cummings
1989 (14603)
This book looks beyond traditional approaches to organizational transition, offering a strategy for developing organizations that enables them to learn not only how to adjust to the dynamic environment in which they exist, but also how to achieve a higher level of performance. This strategy assumes that change is a learning process: the goal is continually refined as organizational members learn how to function more effectively and respond to dynamic conditions in their environment.

### Power and Organization Development:
### Mobilizing Power to Implement Change
Larry E. Greiner and Virginia E. Schein
1988 (12185)
This book forges an important collaborative approach between two opposing and often contradictory approaches to management: OD practitioners who espouse a "more humane" workplace without understanding the political realities of getting

things done, and practicing managers who feel comfortable with power but overlook the role of human potential in contributing to positive results.

### Designing Organizations for High Performance
David P. Hanna
1988 (12693)
This book is the first to give insight into the actual processes you can use to translate organizational concepts into bottom-line improvements. Hanna's "how-to" approach shows not only the successful methods of intervention, but also the plans behind them and the corresponding results.

### Process Consultation, Volume 1: Its Role in Organization Development, Second Edition
Edgar H. Schein
1988 (06736)
How can a situation be influenced in the workplace without the direct use of power or formal authority? This book presents the core theoretical foundations and basic prescriptions for effective management.

### Organizational Transitions: Managing Complex Change, Second Edition
Richard Beckhard and Reuben T. Harris
1987 (10887)
This book discusses the choices involved in developing a management system appropriate to the "transition state." It also discusses commitment to change, organizational culture, and increasing and maintaining productivity, creativity, and innovation.

### The Technology Connection: Strategy and Change in the Information Age
Marc S. Gerstein
1987 (12188)
This is a book that guides managers and consultants through crucial decisions about the use of technology for increasing effectiveness and competitive advantage. It provides a useful way to think about information technology, business strategy, and the process of change in organizations.

### Stream Analysis: A Powerful Way to Diagnose and Manage Organizational Change
Jerry I. Porras
1987 (05693)
Drawing on a conceptual framework that helps the reader to better understand organizations, this book shows how to diagnose failings in organizational function-

ing and how to plan a comprehensive set of actions needed to change the organization into a more effective system.

### *Process Consultation, Volume II: Lessons for Managers and Consultants*
Edgar H. Schein
1987 (06744)
This book shows the viability of the process consultation model for working with human systems. Like Schein's first volume on process consultation, the second volume focuses on the moment-to-moment behavior of the manager or consultant rather than the design of the OD program.

### *Managing Conflict: Interpersonal Dialogue and Third-Party Roles, Second Edition*
Richard E. Walton
1987 (08859)
This book shows how to implement a dialogue approach to conflict management. It presents a framework for diagnosing recurring conflicts and suggests several basic options for controlling or resolving them.

### *Pay and Organization Development*
Edward E. Lawler
1981 (03990)
This book examines the important role that reward systems play in organization development efforts. By combining examples and specific recommendations with conceptual material, it organizes the various topics and puts them into a total systems perspective. Specific pay approaches such as gainsharing, skill-based pay, and flexible benefits are discussed, and their impact on productivity and the quality of work life is analyzed.

### *Work Redesign*
J. Richard Hackman and Greg R. Oldham
1980 (02779)
This book is a comprehensive, clearly written study of work design as a strategy for personal and organizational change. Linking theory and practical technologies, it develops traditional and alternative approaches to work design that can benefit both individuals and organizations.

*Organizational Dynamics: Diagnosis and Intervention*
John P. Kotter
1978 (03890)
This book offers managers and OD specialists a powerful method of diagnosing organizational problems and of deciding when, where, and how to use (or not use) the diverse and growing number of organizational improvement tools that are available today. Comprehensive and fully integrated, the book includes many different concepts, research findings, and competing philosophies and provides specific examples of how to use the information to improve organizational functioning.

*Career Dynamics: Matching Individual and Organizational Needs*
Edgar H. Schein
1978 (06834)
This book studies the complexities of career development from both an individual and an organizational perspective. Changing needs throughout the adult life cycle, interaction of work and family, and integration of individual and organizational goals through human resource planning and development are all thoroughly explored.

*Matrix*
Stanley M. Davis and Paul Lawrence
1977 (01115)
This book defines and describes the matrix organization, a significant departure from the traditional "one man-one boss" management system. The author notes that the tension between the need for independence (fostering innovation) and order (fostering efficiency) drives organizations to consider a matrix system. Among the issues addressed are reasons for using a matrix, methods for establishing one, the impact of the system on individuals, its hazards, and what types of organizations can use a matrix system.

*Feedback and Organization Development: Using Data-Based Methods*
David A. Nadler
1977 (05006)
This book addresses the use of data as a tool for organizational change. It attempts to bring together some of what is known from experience and research and to translate that knowledge into useful insights for those who are thinking about using data-based methods in organizations. The broad approach of the text is to treat a whole range of questions and issues considering the various uses of data as an or-

ganizational change tool.

## Designing Complex Organizations
Jay Galbraith
1973 (02559)
This book attempts to present an analytical framework of the design of organizations that apply lateral decision processes or matrix forms. These forms have become pervasive in all types of organizations, yet there is little systematic public knowledge about them. This book helps fill this gap.

## Organization Development: Strategies and Models
Richard Beckhard
1969 (00448)
This book is written for managers, specialists, and students of management who are concerned with the planning of organization development programs to resolve the dilemmas brought about by a rapidly changing environment. Practiced teams of interdependent people must spend real time improving their methods of working, decision making, and communicating, and a planned, managed change is the first step toward effecting and maintaining these improvements.

## Organization Development: Its Nature, Origins, and Prospects
Warren G. Bennis
1969 (00523)
This primer on OD is written with an eye toward the people in organizations who are interested in learning more about this educational strategy as well as for those practitioners and students of OD who may want a basic statement both to learn from and to argue with. The author treats the subject with a minimum of academic jargon and a maximum of concrete examples and others' experience.

## Developing Organizations: Diagnosis and Action
Paul R. Lawrence and Jay W. Lorsch
1969 (04204)
This book is a personal statement of the author's evolving experience, through research and consulting, in the work of developing organizations. The text presents the authors' overview of organization development, then proceeds to examine the issues at each of three critical interfaces: the organization-environment interface, the group-group interface, and the individual-organization interface, including brief examples of work on each. The text concludes by pulling the themes together in a set of conclusions about organizational development issues as they present themselves to practicing managers.

# About the Authors

Christopher G. Worley (Ph.D., University of Southern California) is Associate Professor of Business Strategy at Pepperdine University's School of Business and Management. He teaches strategic management in the MBA program and is on the core faculty of Pepperdine University's Master of Science in Organization Development (MSOD) program. Prior to his appointment at Pepperdine University, he taught business strategy, organization theory, and project management at the University of San Diego and the University of Southern California. Chris' consulting efforts are focused on the formulation and implementation of large-scale strategic changes, including the development of new strategies, strategic change planning, structural change, performance management systems change, team building, sociotechnical work redesign, and change evaluation. Chris and Dave Hitchin are collaborating to offer strategic change consulting and seminars, and in partnership with Organizational Technologies, Inc., he has consulted to organizations in the public utility, health care, entertainment, high technology, publishing, and financial services industry.

In addition to his teaching and consulting work, he has co-authored (with Thomas G. Cummings) the sixth edition of *Organization Development and Change* (West, 1997). He has published articles on strategic change and organization design in the *Journal of Organization Behavior,* the *International Journal of Public Administration,* and the *Project Management Journal.* He has also presented scholarly papers at the Academy of Management, the Western Academy of Management, the Western Social Sciences Association, and the Strategic Planning Forum.

Chris is currently the Director of Pepperdine University's MSOD Program and continuing his research on strategic change and organization.

David E. Hitchin (Ph.D., University of California at Los Angeles) is Professor of Management at Pepperdine University's School of Business and Management. He teaches strategic management and managing strategic change in the Presidential/Key Executive MBA and Master of Science in Organization Development programs. He has also taught at the University of Southern California and the University of Kansas.

In addition to eighteen years at Pepperdine, Dave has extensive experience as both a consultant to management and an executive. As a consultant, he is founder of the Sun Valley Management Institute and ISC2000, two organizations that specialize in helping organizations develop competitive strategies and implement strategic change. Dave works as a shadow consultant to owners and CEOs on issues of strategy and organization change for mid-market and Fortune 500 companies and is partnering with Chris to provide strategic planning and strategic change consulting. As an executive, Dave was Vice-President of Administration for Sunkist Growers, Inc., where he was responsible for worldwide advertising, strategic planning, human resource management, information systems, and the establishment and management of international subsidiaries in Asia and Europe. He has served as Dean of the Undergraduate Business School and Associate Dean of the Graduate School of Business Administration at the University of Southern California. Dave has also served on the board of directors of several companies and was a member of the National Association of Corporate Directors.

Dave is actively researching and lecturing on the concept of "middlaning," a strategy that attempts to achieve a desirable work-life balance while increasing professional effectiveness.

Walter L. Ross (Ph.D., Brigham Young University) is Director of Organizational Research and Development at the Covey Leadership Center in Provo, Utah. At Covey, he is responsible for research on the application of the principles and processes underlying the Seven Habits of Highly Effective People and Principle Centered Leadership as well as for consulting to Fortune 500 clients in organization development, leadership, and organization design.

Prior to Covey, Walt was Professor of Organization Development at Pepperdine University's School of Business and Management and served as Academic Dean. As Director of the Master of Science in Organization Development program for over ten years and a core faculty member for most of its twenty-year history, Walt had a strong influence on the success of the MSOD program. In addition to teaching at Pepperdine, he has taught undergraduate and graduate courses in organization behavior, statistics, and organization development at Brigham Young University, University of Maryland (Europe), Marshall University, and the California State University.

Walt's background in consulting and management includes vice-presidential positions at two multinational consulting firms—Planning Research Corporation and Forecast Systems. He has consulted to start-up, fast growth, governmental, and Fortune 500 companies trying to change their cultures, structures, and other organizational processes.

Walt is currently researching the change processes that enable organizations to deal with contemporary challenges, such as organization designs of the future and how companies can become aware of and adapt to new paradigms of organizing.

# Foreword

The Addison-Wesley Series on Organizational Development originated in the late 1960's when a number of us recognized that the rapidly growing field of "OD" was not well understood or well defined. We also recognized that there was no one OD philosophy, and hence one could not at that time write a textbook on the theory and practice of OD, but one could make clear what various practitioners were doing under that label. So the original six books launched what has since become a continuing enterprise, the essence of which was to allow different authors to speak for themselves instead of trying to summarize under one umbrella what was obviously a rapidly growing and highly diverse field.

By the early 1980s, the series included nineteen titles. OD was growing by leaps and bounds, and it was expanding into all kinds of organizational areas and technologies of intervention. By this time, many textbooks existed as well that tried to capture core concepts of the field, but we felt that diversity and innovation were still the more salient aspects of OD.

Now as we move towards the end of the century, our series includes over forty titles, and we are beginning to see some real convergence in the underlying assumptions of OD. As we observe how different professionals working in different kinds of organizations and occupational communities make their case, we will see that we are still far from having a single "theory" of organizational development. Yet, a set of common assumptions is surfacing. We are beginning to see patterns in what works and what does not work, and we are becoming more articulate about these patterns. We are also seeing the field increasingly connected to other organizational sciences and disciplines such as information technology, coordination theory, and organization theory. In the early 1990s, we saw several important themes described with Ciampa's *Total Quality* showing the important link to employee involvement in continuous improvement; Johansen et al.'s *Leading Business Teams* exploring the important arena of electronic information tools for teamwork; Tjosvold's *The Conflict-Positive Organization* showing how conflict management can turn conflict into constructive action; Hirschhorn's *Managing in the New Team Environment* building bridges to group psychodynamic theory; and Bushe and Shani's *Parallel Learning Structures* providing an integrative theory for large-scale organizational change.

We continue this trend with four revisions and three new books. Burke has taken his highly successful *Organization Development* into new realms with an updating and expansion. Galbraith has updated and enlarged his classic theory of how information management is at the heart of organization design with his new edition entitled *Competing with Flexible Lateral Organizations*. And Dyer has written an important third edition of his classic book on *Team Building*. In addition, Rashford and Coghlan have introduced the important concept of levels of organizational complexity as a basis for intervention theory in their book entitled *The Dynamics of Organizational Levels*. Woodworth and Meek in *Creating Labor-Management Partnerships* take us into the critical realm of how OD can help in labor relations, an area that's of increasing importance as productivity issues become critical for global competitiveness. Organization development is making important links with related fields. In *Integrated Strategic Change* by Worley, Hitchin and Ross, they powerfully demonstrate how the field of OD must be linked to the field of strategy by reviewing the role of OD at each stage of the strategy planning and implementation process. Finally, an important link to organizational learning is provided by a new version of the classic book by Argyris and Schön entitled *Organizational Learning II: Theory, Method, and Practice*.

We welcome these revisions and new titles and will continue to explore the various frontiers of organization development with additional titles as we identify themes that are relevant to the ever more difficult problem of helping organizations to remain effective in an increasingly turbulent environment.

*New York, New York*                                            Richard H. Beckhard
*Cambridge, Massachusetts*                                  Edgar H. Schein

# Preface

This book is about strategic change and how firms can improve their performance and effectiveness. Its unique contribution is in describing how organization development can assist in the effort. **Strategic change** is defined as a type of organization change that realigns an organization's strategy, structure, and process to fit within a new competitive context. It is substantive and systemic and therefore differs from traditional organization development that produces incremental improvements, addresses only one system at a time, or does not intend to increase firm-level performance.

As a type of organization change, strategic change is occurring all the time. Organizations that survive over long periods are always adjusting their strategies and structures in response to environmental change. However, recognizing the substantive nature of strategic change, we believe it should not be left to chance variation, but rather executed with direction, conviction, and consistency. What is significant about past attempts at designing and implementing *intentional* strategic change is that important and available insights about how organizations grow and change have not been given equal standing with the economic, financial, and content-oriented issues associated with traditional strategic planning. Typical descriptions of strategic change dwell on the changes in products, the structures, and the number of laid-off employees but rarely describe how the senior management team made these difficult decisions. Although it has struggled for relevance, the field and practice of organization development (OD) provides this much needed input.

### Purpose of the Book
With the insights provided by organization development, we intend this book to describe a strategic change process that helps managers decide *when and how* to alter fundamental aspects of their strategic

orientations—the constellation of strategy, structure, and processes that help an organization to achieve its goals. While a considerable amount of research and practice exists regarding how to manage an organization's current strategic orientation, there is a dearth of research and reported practice on *when and how* to change it. We call the process of moving from one strategic orientation to another *integrated strategic change*. Integrated strategic change describes how substantive changes to strategy and organization design can be successfully formulated and implemented through the application of planned change and organization development principles. These principles concern the process and pace of change, emphasize the human systems implications of change, and provide insights into managing and controlling different organizational structures and forms. This book is based on the belief that credible, content-experienced organization development practitioners are in the best position to guide and shape this effort.

### Why We Wrote This Book

We wrote this book because we saw an incredible opportunity to integrate OD's process and change orientation with strategy's traditional content orientation. An important reason for OD's traditional exclusion from the process lies in the historical definitions and self-perceptions of the field of organization development. For the most part, OD is content neutral. Its strength comes from an understanding of the change process, not any particular content area, such as organizational structure, generic strategies (for example, low cost or differentiation), or work design. We believe, like many other OD practitioners, that OD has been losing relevance to business executives and organizations seeking changed performance, not just process facilitation. We see too few quality attempts to integrate the benefits of participation, process, and systems thinking of OD into the more substantive theories of business, such as strategy, total quality management, and organization design.

In fact, the situation is probably getting worse. Rather than trying to integrate "soft asset" OD tools with the "hard asset" disciplines, there is a disturbing trend, especially among OD practitioners, to say that any change they are working on is "strategic change." Under this guise, implementing self-regulating work groups, team building with senior managers, and providing outplacement services during restructuring are being called strategic change (Mintzberg and Westley, 1992).

We believe this notion should be challenged and clarified because it muddies an already cloudy pool of strategic change definitions. The essence of strategy is driving firm performance. If OD interventions are strategic, then OD should be able to show better how its efforts have contributed to organizational performance, not just organizational effectiveness (which it has a tough enough time with). While we understand the needs of many OD practitioners to gain respectability in a field that is battling a history of irrelevancy, we believe OD should not attempt to gain relevance by relabeling its tool kit. What OD should do is involve itself in the life and death issues that help organizations live, thrive, and survive. Clearly one motivation for writing this book is that we believe OD can and should play a value-added role in places where it traditionally has not been used.

### Target Audience

We wrote this book with three audiences in mind, only one of which might be considered traditional from an OD perspective. The first is the OD practitioner, human resource manager, or executive who often reads the Addison-Wesley Series on Organization Development. Many of the change processes, team-oriented activities, and action-planning steps will be quite familiar to them. But the substantive area in which these are applied may seem quite foreign. The area of strategic management is often new ground for the typical OD practitioner. While these practitioners have often heard of "Porter's stuff," helped a group develop a "mission statement," or diagnosed a large system, many of the concepts we present in this book are new and unfamiliar. Further, OD practitioners often have an ethical reticence about becoming involved in strategic planning. OD is not strategy, the argument goes, so practitioners should not get involved in content areas they are unfamiliar with or apply processes that are irrelevant to the formulation and implementation of strategy.

The second audience is the line manager or chief executive who has considerable responsibility for the performance and character of their organization. To these people, the concepts of strategic positioning, goals and objectives, and functional integration of policies are familiar turf. However, while many line managers have been through "team building" and are aware of something called "OD," they generally have not been given the tools or guidance to help them apply OD concepts to improve organization performance.

Finally, we see this book as a potential adjunct to business policy, strategic management, organization theory, or management courses. Most strategy texts are handcuffed by the "formulation and implementation" paradigm that separates doing from thinking. While rational and easy to teach, such a framework does not provide students with an accurate picture of how strategic change really occurs. Thus the models and processes presented here can be used after the traditional coverage of strategic content and are an easy way to introduce notions of strategic change and implementation. In organization theory or management courses, the book can serve as a relevant primer to organization change. Our hope is that our teaching colleagues will imbue the processes described here with the substantive content of business and help these subjects come alive for students.

### The History of This Book

This book has a long history. Its genesis can be traced to changes in the Master of Science in Organization Development (MSOD) program at Pepperdine University. MSOD is the preeminent training ground for OD practitioners. Early versions of the program were built on a solid grounding in group dynamics and change process expertise, but little in the way of real content. Discussions between Richard Beckhard, Edgar Schein, guest speakers, and the MSOD faculty—in particular, David Hitchin and Walter Ross—led to the recognition that OD could play an important and relevant role in shaping business strategies. The program was redesigned in 1987 to include courses in organization design, strategic management, and the management of strategic change.

The integrated strategic change model presented in this book was originally developed by David Hitchin and Walter Ross as part of their work with the MSOD program. Full credit for the creation of this model goes to them. As the book began to take form, Hitchin and Ross invited Chris Worley to bring to the book the most recent thinking in strategy and organization change. This book is the result of that collaboration. Our hope is that it not only represents a model that has been tried and tested but also reflects the latest thinking in strategic change.

### A Word about the Examples

A key feature of the books in the Addison-Wesley Series in Organization Development are the examples that demonstrate the application of key concepts and models. The efforts of two organizations are featured throughout the book. They have successfully grappled with the full range of strategic change issues implied by the model. The first organization is a hospital system located in the Rocky Mountain region. Hospitals are an important sector of the economy that is faced with substantive changes in regulatory requirements, supplier issues, technology, and service delivery. The second organization is a publisher of legal information. The firm (which itself is owned by a larger organization) and one of its key subsidiaries were going through the process of strategic change at about the same time. The key issue here, as will be described in more detail later in the book, was a technological change that threatened very basic assumptions about how to be successful in the legal publishing business.

However, as we shall demonstrate, the model can be broken down or modularized. There is no necessary requirement that the model be followed in its entirety to be useful. Specific activities or processes within the model can be used to address particular strategic problems or issues. Thus, in addition to the two featured organizations, other firms that have implemented different parts of the integrated strategic change model are also described.

The examples in this book represent a slightly different focus than is typical in most OD books. Typical strategy examples describe that a new product was developed in half the normal time or that a new market was entered by using a particular approach and that sales increased by X percent. In other words, strategy examples are very content oriented. OD examples, on the other hand, are process oriented. They described how Manager A saw a problem or opportunity, gathered people together, applied a particular intervention, and implemented it. Our effort here has attempted to balance these two perspectives by providing a rich description of the process that is steeped in the strategic issue being addressed.

### *Outline of the Book*

This book is divided into nine chapters. In Chapter 1, we describe the book's objectives. These include the development of a practical model that integrates the strengths of strategic management and organization development and develops organizational capabilities to implement strategic change over and over again. We argue that the latter objective will contribute to increased organizational competitiveness. We also discuss the value-added role that OD can play in discussions of strategic change. In Chapter 2, we extend this discussion by focusing on the definition and dimensions of strategic change, providing a brief overview of the integrated strategic change model, and describing a short case example of the model in use.

In Chapters 3 through 8, we present the four steps involved in the integrated strategic change process. Chapters 3 and 4 concern the process of strategic analysis, the crucial first step associated with diagnosing the organization's current strategic orientation. Chapter 3 describes how to assess the organization's readiness to carry out strategic change and the process of determining the key values, issues, and priorities that will guide the diagnostic activities. Chapter 4 focuses on the process of diagnosing the organization's current strategic orientation, including its mission, goals and objectives, strategic intent, and distinctive and dominant competences. It includes a description of the strategic management and organization development tools necessary to carry out this diagnostic process.

In Chapters 5 and 6, we describe step two or strategy making. Chapter 5 outlines the process of visioning and choosing among several strategic change alternatives. Chapter 6 discusses the content and process issues associated with designing the organization's desired future strategic orientation. In these chapters, we discuss the development of the organization's strategic vision and the selection of the type of strategic change that best fits the organization's circumstances. Then, we talk about the formulation of the appropriate changes in strategy and/or organization design. We also discuss the role different stakeholders can play during this crucial phase of the process, paying particular attention to senior management's role and responsibility.

In Chapters 7 and 8, we define and discuss the development and implementation of the strategic change plan. More than a strategic plan, the strategic change plan describes the organizational activities, responsibilities, resources, timelines, and commitments necessary for carrying out strategic change.

In the final chapter, Chapter 9, we reflect on the process of strategic change, its implications for industrial competitiveness and survival, and the prospects of improving organizations through an integrated process. We utilize the integrated strategic change model to discuss how organizations should begin to develop the capability to change their orientations over and over again.

### Acknowledgments

Several people have helped us bring this book to life. In particular, MSOD students from Pepperdine University have challenged and questioned the model and its application. First, the entire CHI class reviewed the manuscript and provided us with brutally honest feedback. Their passionate response put some much needed polish on several sections. Second, several students also provided detailed comments on earlier manuscripts. These include David Clark, Judy Kingsley, Dan Dyble, Shelley Brinkman, Laura Harvell, and Sarah Horsman. The book also benefited from discussions with the MSOD faculty: Bob Canady, David Jamieson, Miriam Lacey, Kurt Motamedi, Joanne Preston, and Pat Williams.

We are very grateful to the following individuals who commented on the manuscript: Ed Lawler, Larry Greiner, and Len Schlesinger. In addition, Foster Mobley of Organizational Technologies, Inc., reviewed several drafts of the manuscript and provided valuable suggestions for improving its message. He was also one of the first practitioners to adopt the process. Many of the examples in this book are based on client organizations of his that used the model. The hospital and legal publisher that are the topics of the cases used throughout the book are two of Foster's clients who agreed to try out the integrated strategic change process.

The three of us are blessed with a strong support system. Anyone who has written a book knows how much it affects the family. Our wives, Debbie, Jill, and Sandy, deserve perhaps the biggest thanks.

Finally, many thanks go to Ed Schein, Dick Beckhard, and the people at Addison-Wesley who did not give up on our ideas.

*Carlsbad, California*                                            C.G.W.
*Sun Valley, Idaho*                                              D.E.H.
*Provo, Utah*                                                    W.L.R.

# Contents

# Integrated Strategic Change
## How OD Builds Competitive Advantage

# 1

# Organization Development, Strategic Change, and Industrial Competitiveness

When we begin talking about our interest in integrating strategy and organization development (OD), we get looks that range from "you must be crazy" to "well, of course, it's only natural." This book is primarily aimed at the "you must be crazy" crowd because the truth is, strategy and strategic planning have not lived up to their potentials. What's really funny is that while we agree with this, it is not our conclusion. It's the conclusion of no less a student of strategy than Henry Mintzberg (1994). Understanding such a sweeping statement and why we think an "OD Perspective" provides the elusive "missing ingredient" requires knowledge of how strategic planning is traditionally applied and the context of its application.

In response to global competition, major changes in industry structures, and increased demand for speed, quality, and flexibility, organizations have merged, acquired, restructured, downsized, implemented total quality management (TQM), formed strategic alliances, and opened global markets. Unfortunately, these initiatives represent new territory to many firms, and although strategic concepts help to explain firm behavior, it does not help them understand how to implement these changes. For example, mergers create redundant positions and systems, changes in reporting relationships and reward systems, and often a collision of cultures. Downsizing heightens insecurity and political behavior. A new focus on quality and customer relationships means changes in policies, cultural values, work procedures and processes, relationships between departments, and interactions with customers and suppliers. These concomitants of strategic change are not addressed by traditional strategic planning, which simply concerns itself with whether some action makes financial and strategic sense. While larger organizations and firms operating in more turbulent environments are more likely to have faced radical change, this doesn't make the process any easier.

Further, when these strategic moves are countered by competitors, traditional organizations are uncertain about how to respond. Having little or no experience in implementing new strategies, they lack a basis for planning and decision making. There is no latent, embedded process for guiding change. As a result, they are uncertain about what they should hold on to and what they should abandon. They are looking for leadership and expertise to help them through these turbulent times.

This is the major challenge management faces in today's competitive environment. It is no longer enough to manage the external positioning of the firm. Rather, both short-term and long-term performance requires executives to manage external and internal considerations simultaneously and to comprehend both the challenges in the marketplace and those within their organizations. They also must develop and implement successful business strategies that strengthen the organization and increase the level of motivation and commitment of the people who are responsible for implementation.

When all the dust has settled, the driving force behind this book is our vision that a change process that integrates strategy with OD will improve the long-term competitiveness of organizations. To realize that vision, we lay in this chapter the important groundwork for our discussion. First, we explore our rationale for proposing that strategy and OD should and can be integrated. The result of this integration is a model (described in Chapter 2) that shows how an organization's strategic orientation[1] can evolve over time. Second, we argue that the *capability* to change a firm's strategic orientation over and over again is a truly sustainable competitive advantage. Finally, we lay out what we believe to be the essence of an "OD Perspective" and how such a perspective can contribute to the management of strategic change.

---

[1]Strategic orientation is itself an integrated concept that proposes that a firm's strategy cannot be divorced from its organization design; that is, strategy, structure, and process are an integrated whole. The research by Tushman and Romanelli (1985) holds that a strategic orientation is the constellation of a firm's strategy, power distributions, structures, and control systems. For simplicity, we use the term strategic orientation to refer to the firm's strategy and the organization design that supports it.

## Why OD and Strategy Should Be Integrated

An important objective of this book is to describe how processes of strategic management, such as formulating and implementing new strategic orientations, can be improved by integrating principles of OD. For some, strategy and OD are two distinct and antithetical perspectives. Traditional approaches to strategy and business policy, for example, are externally focused, content oriented, static, and concerned with financial performance (Porter, 1991; Rumelt, Schendel, and Teece, 1991). Its intellectual heritage in economics, finance, and marketing produces an external orientation that manifests itself in discussions of industry and market structure and product/service positioning vis-à-vis competitors. This same heritage also results in a content orientation that focuses on goals and objectives, product/service characteristics, and resource allocation policies (for example, advertising-to-sales ratios). It also focuses on the alignment of strategy and structure at a particular point in time and explores the impact of those relationships on current performance.

OD, on the other hand, is internally focused, process oriented, dynamic, and concerned with effectiveness (Cummings and Worley, 1993). It deals with the process of planned change. Its intellectual heritage is in the behavioral sciences and organizational theory. This heritage results in a focus on the people and groups that operate inside organizations and on the processes associated with teamwork, change, and integration. Because OD focuses on change, it is naturally concerned with dynamics, that is, how organizations and organizational behavior evolve over time. Finally, the behavioral science and organizational theory perspectives are concerned with improving organizational effectiveness in the broadest sense of the term.

While these differences may appear large, we believe the two perspectives have more in common than meets the eye. Traditional business policy and competitive strategy are primarily concerned with the relationship between an organization and its environment. There are two aspects to this concern. The first involves crafting relationships among strategy, structure, and process that maintain the organization's position in its environment in order to maximize performance. This is a difficult task that is more dynamic than it sounds because the organization's relevant environment and its strategic orientation are always changing. For example, as consumer preferences change, the marketing research function feeds information to the research and development (R&D) department, which translate needs into product features. In turn, the new products need advertising support, promotional materials, and manufacturing capacity. Each of these activities must be balanced and integrated to result in improved performance. Another example demonstrates the breadth of the strategic management concept. As workforce diversity increases, old "one-size-fits-all" human resource practices give way to flexible policies that respect individual differences (Jamieson and O'Mara, 1991). Firms that embrace diversity as an opportunity will have advantages over other firms in attracting and retaining skilled labor or finding the appropriate mix of labor to meet their objectives. In each of these examples, the organization alters policies and procedures that adapt its existing strategic orientation to be better aligned with a changing aspect of its environment. Even though the organization's basic strategies and structures have not changed, change is clearly occurring.

Second, traditional business policy and competitive strategy are concerned with understanding when and how to fundamentally alter the organization's strategies, structures, and processes. All organizations at some time must abandon their strategic orientations and reinvent themselves. For example, as important new product and process technologies become available, the organization may adopt and implement them. If it does, a new strategy based on the characteristics of new products or markets often emerges, a new plant is started to produce the new line, new employees with different skills and competences are employed, and a new structure is implemented. This scenario may well describe the process that General Motors (GM) went through in launching its Saturn line of cars, that record firms went through as compact disks became commercialized, or that telecommunications firms are going through as computer, video, and fiber optics technologies converge. These changes differ fundamentally from the incremental changes associated with traditional strategic management. They involve important and substantive alterations in strategy, structure, and process that require extensive planning, analysis, and direction. Less radically but more frequently, organizations also need to substantively adapt their internal structures and systems or revise their strategies.

The activities associated with either incremental adjustments or strategic reorientations clearly occur over time and deal with issues of change. However, the largest criticism of strategic management is the difficulty in getting good strategies implemented. Traditional strategy formulation and implementation approaches primarily involve describing the content of change—the "what," not the process or the "how." OD suggests that such changes can be accomplished in ways that minimize costs and human frustration and maximize efficiency and human potential. Unfortunately, OD principles rarely are used in strategy implementation.

This is slowly changing, however. In fact, each perspective is beginning to embrace concepts of the other. The very concept of strategic management, as distinct from business policy or competitive strategy, has recognized the dynamic aspects of managing a strategic orientation over time. Within strategic management, for example, the problems associated with good strategic plans that gather dust and fail to get implemented have produced increased interest in strategy implementation, strategy making processes, and top management team dynamics (Pettigrew, 1992; Hart, 1992; Hambrick, 1981). Within OD, the focus on human process issues, often to the exclusion of important content issues, restricted its use to a rather narrow set of applications and limited its relevance (Huber, Sutcliffe, Miller, and Glick, 1992). This, too, is changing as OD attempts to become oriented more toward content issues and strategy (Cummings and Worley, 1993; Jelenik and Litterer, 1988; Buller, 1988). An integrated approach to strategic change—one that looks at both internal and external issues, appreciates the importance of process and content, and examines organizational effectiveness in all its forms—is better than separate approaches. Thus we believe there is a natural place for OD within the paradigm of strategic management and that integration of the two perspectives is near.

## Change and Competitiveness

A second, and in some ways more important, objective of this book is to provide organizations with a long-term source of competitive advantage: the capability to create and implement strategic change over and over again. Understanding this objective requires understanding the sources, nature, and limits of competitive advantage.

### *What Is a Sustainable Competitive Advantage?*

**Sustainable competitive advantage** is an organization's ability to garner profits from valuable resources over time. It is the *sine qua non* of strategic management. By definition, organizations making a profit or surviving have some sort of advantage. These advantages may be external—such as product technologies, market share, brand image, and access to distribution channels—or internal—such as a quality-oriented culture, learning curve advantages, or specialized skills. In the short run, sustainability is a function of how easy it is for one firm to imitate another firm's competitive advantage (Prahalad and Hamel, 1990). An advantage that is easy to imitate is not sustainable. For example, although the Miller Brewing Company was the first to offer "lite" beer, the advantage was quickly imitated by other brewers. Miller's innovation earned it significant profits for a short time, but the advantage was not sustainable because the "lite" technology could be imitated rather easily. This same scenario is being played out today with "dry," "cold-filtered," and "ice-brewed" beers. In contrast, an advantage that is difficult to imitate, such as Nutrasweet's patent-protected formula during the 1980s, is sustainable. The inability to challenge Nutrasweet in the artificial sweetener market allowed the firm to earn monopoly profits. Not until 1993, when the patent expired, did Nutrasweet have to defend its advantage.

Managers and executives are paying more attention to the sources of competitive advantage. Obviously, if they can understand and develop a sustainable advantage, they may be able to earn substantial profits over a period of years. One of the more interesting findings is that even the most powerful sources of external advantage have their roots in internal resources (Grant, 1992). The source of an innovative and successful product is often a set of creative R&D engineers. In the mid-1980s, for example, a large defense contractor received almost every helicopter weapons development project offered by the government because it employed an engineer who was familiar with the technology that allowed pilots to aim their weaponry by looking at a target. This one human resource accounted for a majority of the firm's competitive advantage. As a result, there is renewed interest in understanding an organization's strategic resources and in developing them into distinctive competences and capabilities.

For example, in *The Ultimate Advantage* (1992), Ed Lawler argues that the best source of sustainable competitive advantage is the organization's design. The difficulty of aligning structures and systems with each other and in support of the organization's goals and strategies suggest that its accomplishment would represent a sustainable advantage. These structures and systems include rewards, work design, technical core processes, information systems, performance appraisal, and decision-making authority. Fully implementing a TQM process, for example, appears to be sufficiently difficult (current failure rates appear to be in the 50-percent range), so its success can be considered a sustainable advantage. The advantage is sustainable because it cannot be imitated easily. In addition, a firm with

TQM can create continuous improvements in a variety of performance dimensions that traditionally managed competitors cannot. If these traditionally managed firms do eventually implement TQM, they will be subject to a sustained cost disadvantage as the early mover travels ahead of them down the experience curve.

### The Ability to Change IS a Competitive Advantage

In the long run, however, any source of competitive advantage, while salient and important for a period of time, eventually shifts to other sources. Patent protection runs out, consumer preferences change, technological discontinuities occur, or the cost of making an additional quality improvement exceeds the benefits. The resources that once conferred an advantage become irrelevant or depreciate in value. Thus even sustainable advantages may provide performance enhancements only for a given time period.

We conclude that the only truly *sustainable* competitive advantage is the capability to make the transition from one set of strategies, structures, and processes that exploit an old advantage to another strategic orientation that exploits a new advantage—in short, the capability to design and implement strategic change.

While many authors have discussed competitive advantage and strategic change, few have argued that the latter is the best example of the former. Our second objective attempts to address that gap and to help organizations create a truly sustainable competitive advantage through a model and a process that shows managers *when and how* to make fundamental changes in their firm's strategies, structures, and processes. We believe that such an ability is at the heart of revitalizing U.S. industrial and organizational competitiveness. The firm with the capacity not only to manage its current strategic orientation but also to change orientations and adapt to a new context of effectiveness is more competitive than one that is unable to make that shift. While few people will deny this logic, the issue is that most firms cannot make the change.

General Electric (GE), Ford, Hewlett-Packard, IBM, GM, and Sears provide recent and potent contrasts in strategic change and well exemplify the need for a practical book on the subject. These organizations are exemplars of capitalism, big business, and state-of-the-art management practice. Each faced in the 1980s long-term trends and short-term changes in technological frontiers, industry structure, competitor behavior, and consumer preferences. While GE, Ford, and Hewlett-Packard adapted, IBM, GM, and Sears did not. GE, Ford, and Hewlett-Packard engaged in large-scale transformations that altered corporate and business strategies, structures, and systems. As a result, they not only maintained or expanded their domestic positions in a tough recession, they also expanded globally.

But IBM, GM, and Sears, despite similar conditions, failed to create the strategic and organizational changes necessary to sustain their pre-eminent positions. Instead of expanding and growing in the early 1990s, they lost market share, reputation, money, and employee loyalty. IBM alone lost 67 percent of its market value between 1987 and 1993 and was forced by angry stockholders and its board of directors to hire an "outsider" (Sherman, 1993).

These and other examples amply demonstrate the problem. Despite well-developed and sophisticated strategic planning processes, many managers exposed to and trained in strategic management, and a plethora of good strategies from which to choose, organizations are often unable to implement a chosen strategy well. As a result, the full benefit of these plans are never realized. Worse, the plans and strategies often remain "on the shelf" and unimplemented. It is our belief that competitive advantage in the 1990s and beyond will come from a firm's ability to both formulate new strategies and implement them well *over and over again.* Understanding and then acquiring such a capability, we argue, begins by approaching the tasks of strategic management with an "OD Perspective."

## The OD Perspective

To understand how OD can play a value-added role in strategic management, consider the requirements of superior performance: good strategies implemented well. The first requirement is formulation of a good strategy. This is, we argue, an increasingly likely occurrence. During the late 1970s and all of the 1980s, the MBA was the holy grail of graduate degrees and millions of baby boomers flocked to business schools, both prestigious and lowly, to begin the quest for fame and fortune. Strategy, the capstone course in these programs, was the most celebrated of all classes. As these graduates came to occupy and influence senior management, strategic planning processes and strategic planning departments gained status, power, and political favor. More and more, large and small organizations alike have access to the models of strategic planning taught in the business schools. Thus the probability that any firm can develop and choose from among several viable strategic alternatives is enhanced. It is becoming less likely over time that a firm has a "poor" strategy, although firms and strategic planners do make mistakes.

### OD and Strategy Implementation

As more and more firms generate better and better strategies, *superior* performance will be more often correlated with good implementation, the most neglected area of strategy. Thus while most people will accept as axiomatic that success is a function of good strategy implemented well, it is implementation processes that will determine *superior* performance. Given the relative lack of attention by firms to implementation processes in strategic management, OD's strengths in planning and managing change offer great potential to organizations.

As implementation becomes an increasingly important aspect of competitiveness and sustainable advantage, the need for a process approach to strategy also increases. In fact, this explains why more and more attention in the strategy literature is being given to issues such as power and political behavior, strategic decision making, top management team behavior, and organization design. Implementation's traditional role in strategy, in line with its overall static orientation, has been to specify the structures and processes necessary to support a given strategy. In the main, strategy implementation has *not* been concerned with how to bring about the alignment (see, for example, Galbraith and Kazanjian, 1986). These issues are important areas of research and practice in OD. Not surprisingly, there has been an increasing number of calls for more process-oriented strategy research as well as more calls for OD to be more strategic.

In short, strategic management processes are missing what we refer to as the **OD Perspective**. Specifically, the OD Perspective emphasizes the following:

- A long-term, processual, and dynamic approach to organizational evolution
- The systemic effects of organizational decisions
- The roles that people and organization design can play as competitive advantages
- The development of individuals and the organization in ways that fit the organization's strategic direction
- Processes that produce effective problem solving and decision making, align individual and organizational goals, and result in high levels of motivation, commitment, and accountability for outcomes
- The ability to create, respond to, and manage change.

Bringing the OD Perspective to strategic management assures that organizational capabilities, work processes, and human resource issues are considered along with strategic and goal-oriented concerns. Our experience with the Integrated Strategic Change process (discussed in Chapter 2) suggests that successful organizations have adapted to this perspective in their strategic management processes.

### The Value-Added of OD

When a firm incorporates the OD Perspective into the strategic management process, a more integrated approach to strategic change results. More specifically, the OD Perspective brings three types of expertise to the strategic management process that improve its effectiveness:

1. Subject matter expertise
2. Process expertise
3. Intervention expertise

The first is **subject matter expertise.** Traditional approaches to strategy have focused on the content of those strategies and not on the "softer" areas of change management, organizational diagnosis, group dynamics, organizational behavior, and human resource management. Each of these areas helps to improve the implementation of any given strategy.

The OD Perspective also brings **process expertise**—the ability to understand, predict, and control how organizations successfully implement change. Such expertise includes knowledge and skills associated with group and team development, organizational evolution, and transition management. This knowledge will be extremely helpful in elaborating strategic change processes over and above the simple specification of what needs to change.

Finally, the OD Perspective brings **intervention expertise**—the ability to design activities that improve organizational functioning. The whole range of OD interventions, from individual and group/team development to changes in work and organization design, are valuable tools in producing strategic organizational capabilities. While the practice of these interventions is not limited to OD professionals, they can play an important role in the strategic change process.

## Summary

In this chapter, we laid the ground work for our presentation of an integrated strategic change process. First, OD and strategy are really flip sides of the same coin. Strategic management is content oriented and concerned with the relationship between a firm and its environment but is less involved with internal issues. OD is process oriented and concerned with how organizations develop over time and in response to environmental change but is less involved with strategic issues. Their integration yields an approach that appreciates both the content of strategic orientation and the processes of changing from one orientation to another. Second, the capacity to repeatedly change strategic orientations is a sustainable competitive advantage. Because almost all traditional sources of competitive advantage eventually deteriorate, only the ability to change holds the promise of being a truly sustainable advantage. Finally, the OD Perspective can contribute to the development of this capacity and represents a value-added addition to the practice of strategic management.

# 2

# The Integrated Strategic Change Model

Research into the subject of strategic change and our experience with a broad range of organizations has led us to formulate a process approach to strategic management and change. This approach enhances both the ability to achieve a particular strategic orientation and the commitment of organization members to strategic objectives. It enables organizations to produce above average returns as well as to learn and adapt. The learning and adapting allows organizations to remain truly competitive over time, adapting and reorienting themselves appropriately as the business environment changes.

We call this approach **Integrated Strategic Change (ISC)**. It has four key features:

1. It treats the following as one integrated process, not separate, independent activities: formulating strategy and the appropriate organization design, gaining commitment and support for that strategy and design, planning their implementation, executing them, and evaluating their results.

2. It focuses not only on conventional business issues—such as market share, product development, and operations—but also on organizational capabilities, human resources, and organizational changes required to implement specific strategic orientations.

3. It provides for individuals and groups throughout the organization to be involved in meaningful and practical ways in the analysis, planning, and implementation process in order to create a more achievable strategy, maintain the firm's strategic focus, improve coordination and integration within the organization, and create higher levels of shared ownership and commitment.

4. It is a continuous process for developing the firm's capacity to create, manage, and respond effectively to change.

The ISC approach gives equal standing to both the strategic and business issues that define an organization's performance potential and the human and organizational issues that ultimately determine whether that performance is fully realized. The approach integrates the primarily content perspective of strategic management with the process perspective of OD.

This chapter presents the integrated strategic change model. First, we explore three basic dimensions that must be addressed by any strategic change model. Second, we present the model and describe the basic steps. Finally, we conclude with an example of the ISC model in action.

## The Dimensions of Strategic Change

We adopt the following definition:

**Integrated strategic change** is the deliberate, coordinated process that leads radically or gradually to *systemic* realignments between the environment and a firm's strategic orientation and that results in improvements in performance and effectiveness.

This definition, based on the research of Greiner and Bhambri (1989), explicitly and implicitly identifies three dimensions of strategic change:

1. Content
2. Causes and consequences
3. Process

### The Content of Change

There has been much debate over the content of strategic change. Some argue that the label "strategic change" should be applied only to cases in which the organization alters *both* its strategy and organization. Others believe it should apply only when *either* strategy or organization change. Still others argue that the term has no meaning at all. For our purposes, *strategic change* refers to relatively major and systemic shifts in strategic orientation and to changes that improve either strategic or organizational alignment (Nadler and Tushman, 1992). **Strategic alignment** is the firm's positioning within its environment; whether, for example, the firm has achieved the lowest total costs in the industry or differentiated its product or service in the minds of customers. **Organizational alignment** concerns the extent to which the firm's structures and processes support the firm's strategy. For example, a firm attempting to achieve the lowest cost position in the industry would be supported by an organization design that focuses resources on process improvements, carefully tracks expenses in all functions, and rewards managers and employees who demonstrate high levels of efficiency.

## The Causes and Consequences of Change

It is important to know what causes strategic change to occur and what happens as a result. Strategic change theories that do not address issues of cause and consequence are fundamentally flawed (Pettigrew, 1985). Strategic change in any form is a complex organizational response that can be caused by an equally complex set of internal and external conditions. The causes of strategic change, although not specifically referred to in our definition, are practically limitless. Fortunately, they can be arranged into four categories:

1. The transition to a global economy
2. Changing industry structures and competitive conditions
3. Firm performance
4. Stakeholder initiatives

The transition to a global economy provides many opportunities for strategic change. Examples of the tremendous adaptive challenges existing organizations face include a unified Germany, a more capitalistic Russia, the reversion of Hong Kong from British to Chinese rule, the opening of the People's Republic of China, the European Common Market, and a developing North American free trade arena. Because these areas represent new international markets, the regulatory and cultural requirements for operating there are still in flux.

Strategic change has also been associated with changes in competitive conditions within a particular industry. Technological and regulatory changes are drastically altering the financial, airline, telecommunications, and transportation industries. Among the most celebrated causes is technological change—in the form of new products, new manufacturing processes, new service delivery concepts, and information systems—which destroys entry barriers, increases rivalry among firms, alters buyer and supplier bargaining power, and creates viable substitute products and services (Porter, 1980). Regulatory changes within the United States create huge levels of uncertainty. The range of changes and initiatives taking place in the telecommunications industry provide ample evidence that strategic change accompanies regulatory change. Health care reform looms as one of the next great transformational challenges.

A third important source of strategic change is firm performance. The generally accepted view has been that poor performance is an important catalyst for change, whereas high performance is an inhibitor to change. This view has been challenged recently by those who see low firm performance more as a constraint to change than a facilitator. According to this view, change requires resources that are in too short a supply when the firm is experiencing low performance relative to its industry. Medium performance levels, on the other hand, have been shown to facilitate change (Fombrun and Ginsberg, 1988).

Stakeholder initiatives have also played an important role in strategic change. For example, the increased level of education in the work force and the desire for more involvement in decisions that affect work have prodded organizations into high-involvement designs (Lawler, 1986). Self-managed work teams have become an important element of strategy implementation and organization design (Fortune, 1992). Other stakeholders, such as stockholders and senior management, are also an important source of change. Stockholders, gaining power through collective action, are demanding more efficient and more effective organizations. And management succession, especially the influence of insider and outsider appointments to executive positions, is an important and much researched topic in strategic change (Greiner and Bhambri, 1989).

Strategic change also has several outcomes, ranging from incremental improvements to complete turnarounds in performance and effectiveness. We accept as given that firms engaging in strategic change expect improvements in organizational effectiveness. Effectiveness can be viewed from several perspectives, however. Traditionally, strategic management has been most concerned with financial performance in some form, be it measures of profitability (for example, ROA, ROE, ROI), productivity, or growth. OD, on the other hand, is traditionally associated with the "softer" measures of effectiveness, such as employee, job, or stakeholder satisfaction, absenteeism, and the quality of work life. According to the definition of strategic change adopted here, any or all of these could be expected consequences.

## The Process of Change

Finally, definitions of strategic change should describe how change happens. Despite terms like "transformation" and "discontinuous change" that imply almost instantaneous rates of change, the hard truth is that change occurs over time. Strategic change definitions need to address the issues of not only what to change but also how and when to change different elements of a strategic orientation. Currently, there are no clearly accepted strategic change process steps. One proposal suggests that strategic change is initiated by a new, outside CEO brought in to implement change. Shortly after assuming office, the CEO takes actions that solve short-term performance problems and consolidate power. The CEO then develops a consensus among top management on strategic direction and realigns organizational structure, with supporters filling key positions. Finally, leadership responsibility is transferred to middle managers and new systems are implemented to assure consistency in workforce behavior (Greiner and Bhambri, 1989).

Another researcher sees a different pattern. Within the context of internal forces resisting change and external forces promoting change, top management first deciphers their environments and, if insightful, commits to strategic change. In the second phase, the firm revises its strategic posture to gain new competitive advantages at the business level, extends core capabilities at the corporate level, or broadens a network of alliances at the collective level. Finally, managers energize strategic change. This final phase involves redefining the organization's vision, allocating resources toward new directions, modifying organizational systems, and generating commitment among organizational members (Fombrun, 1992).

These two examples demonstrate the difficulty in establishing a strategic change process definition. The first example is primarily concerned with internal processes of power and structure, while the second is primarily concerned with external issues of competitive advantage and positioning. In addition, each differs in the timing and sequence of changes in strategy, structure, vision, and other elements of strategic orientation.

The definition of ISC adopted here suggests that such change occurs because of dramatic shifts in either a firm's environment (industry structure, global competition, stakeholder activism, and so on) or the firm's performance. The ISC model proposed in the next section describes the systemic changes in a firm's strategic orientation. In addition, it proposes that as a result of change, organizational effectiveness (performance, stakeholder satisfaction, and productivity) will improve and that the organization will have learned how to address future changes in its environment.

## Components of the ISC Model

The ISC model is shown in Figure 2.1 (on the next page). This model describes strategic change in terms of a current state, a future state, and a planned sequence of activities that move the firm from where it is to where it wants to be. It is a more specific form of Beckhard and Harris's (1987) transition state model. For example, instead of a generic "current state" or "desired future state" that could apply to any organizational system, these "states" are represented by an organization's strategic orientation, that is, its strategy (S) and supporting organization design factors (O). The ISC model is slightly different in that the strategic change plan (SCP), which documents the activities that will move the organization from its current strategic orientation to its future one, is less a state than a stream of activities. Over time, the desired strategic orientation ($S_2/O_2$) becomes the old strategic orientation and the process is begun again when appropriate.

The ISC approach suggests that the following four steps are involved:

1. Strategic analysis
2. Strategy making
3. Strategic change plan design
4. Strategic change plan implementation

Although the ISC process sounds linear and appears to separate strategy formulation from implementation, just as traditional approaches do, this is more an artifact of writing in two dimensions than philosophy and process. In fact, the success of the ISC process is critically dependent on the strategic analysis and strategy making steps being conducted in such a way that the SCP becomes *de facto*. This results from performing strategic management activities with an OD Perspective and summarizes the value-added contribution of this book. That is, the process of diagnosing a firm's current strategic orientation in Step 1 or envisioning its future in Step 2 is a reality-based, highly participative process that is owned by the various stakeholders

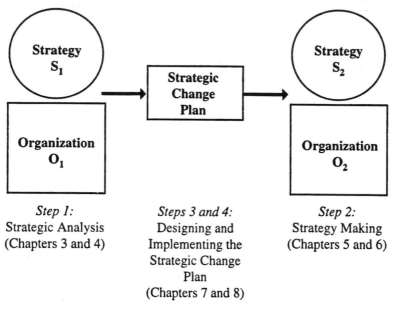

**Figure 2.1**
*The Integrated Strategic Change Model*

of the organization. Such a process orientation, which is lacking in most treatments of strategy formulation, develops commitment to change and increases the probability of building a successful SCP.

These four steps exist in two specific contexts: (1) the firm's industry structure and environment and (2) its performance. Although the model in Figure 2.1 does not show it, firm performance is defined by the environment on the one hand and the firm's strategic orientation on the other. Seeing firm performance as partly determined by industry structure is in keeping with the industrial organization model of strategy (Porter, 1980). But performance is also determined by the firm's strategic orientation, and hence the model suggests that the new strategic orientation, if successfully implemented, increases performance.

### Step One: Strategic Analysis

The ISC process begins with a thorough assessment and diagnosis of the organization's external environment and its current strategic orientation ($S_1/O_1$). The assessment determines the organization's effectiveness and efficiency in meeting present strategic objectives and fulfilling the mission of the enterprise.

Both OD and strategy make substantive contributions to this step in the process. OD, for example, has a long association with diagnostic processes. A diagnostic step is central in most theories of planned change (Lippit, Watson, and Westley, 1954; Burke, 1992) and presumes a model exists to describe how an organization functions and achieves objectives. The purpose of diagnostic activities is to separate symptoms from causes and to focus on the real problems whose solutions will lead to increased effectiveness and performance. OD has tended to use models such as Nadler and Tushman's Congruency Model (1992) or Weisbord's (1976) Six Box Model for organization-level diagnoses. However, such models do not give primacy to strategic issues. For example, strategy is not mentioned in Weisbord's model, while in the Congruency Model, strategy is addressed only in terms of the decisions "that allocate scarce resources against the constraints and opportunities of a given environment" (1992: 47).

We have found that models of strategic orientation are better suited to the ISC process (Tushman and Romanelli, 1985; Miles and Snow, 1978). These models support the belief that a firm's strategies, structures, and processes represent an integrated whole but still can be conveniently broken down into issues of firm strategy and issues of organization design. In this way, substantive content issues such as mission, goals and objectives, and competitive positioning, as well as issues of structure, reward and control systems, performance appraisal, and culture, can be brought to bear on the diagnosis.

It is important to note that we do not place the visioning process in this step. Rather, we believe that visioning should occur after the organization has a clear sense of its strengths and weaknesses. In this way, the organization is less likely to envision a future it can never approach and more likely to develop strategies that can be implemented well. This line of reasoning is in keeping with the emerging resource-based view of strategy (Grant, 1992).

### Step Two: Strategy Making

The strategy making step in the ISC process consists of developing a strategic vision, selecting the appropriate type of strategic change, and designing the future strategic orientation. As a result, the firm formulates either a new strategy ($S_2$) or new organization design

($O_2$) or both. The chosen strategy ($S_2$) describes the products or services to be offered, the market segments to be targeted and served, and the ways those products or services will be positioned to give the organization a competitive advantage. It also includes the various policies necessary for the firm to obtain and keep specified market shares, reach targeted levels of revenue and profitability, and enhance shareholder value. Strategy making, in addition to describing the future strategy, specifies the type of organization ($O_2$) required to support this strategic position. The appropriate organization is defined by the core processes that must be executed well to survive and that distinguish the firm from its competitors. These processes, explained more fully in Chapter 4, are supported by the organization's structural, work, information, and human resource systems. Explicit attention is given to the culture of the firm in terms of its ability to facilitate or constrain achievement of the new strategic orientation.

The strategy making step is dominated by processes of strategy formulation, although they are infused with the OD Perspective. That is, while visioning (discussed in detail in Chapter 5) is primarily associated with leadership and OD, designing future strategic orientations, especially with regard to future strategies, is well understood and specified by strategic management theory and practice.

### Step Three: Strategic Change Plan Design

The SCP documents a carefully thought-out process for moving the organization from its current strategic orientation to the desired future position. The SCP is both externally and internally focused. Externally, the SCP deals with the traditional actions and programs that are a part of every strategic plan, such as how to increase market share, initiate new product development efforts, identify merger or acquisition candidates, implement technology policies, or acquire funding for expansion and modernization.

Internally, the SCP provides guidelines for successful change within the organization by considering power, political alliances, the nature of the organization's culture, and its readiness to support the desired changes. To the extent that the SCP acknowledges the irrational, dysfunctional, and totally human aspects of the organization rather than theoretical abstractions, it becomes the key to successful organizational growth and learning. Operationally, this means the organization does not try to alter everything at once, but rather appreciates the reality of resistance to change. As a result, attention is given to the sequence and pace of change.

### Step Four: Strategic Change Plan Implementation

The final step in the ISC process is the actual implementation of the SCP. This step includes traditional activities such as developing budgets and timetables and assigning responsibility for certain activities and results. But the implementation step also draws on an understanding of individual motivation, group dynamics, and organizational change. The process continuously deals with such organizational issues as alignment, adaptability, participation, and teamwork. Finally, implementing the SCP includes measurement and review activities to assure corrective steps are taken quickly when required and that necessary revisions are made in critical action programs, in budgets and timetables, and even in objectives.

Implementation of the SCP builds the organization's capabilities, enhances individual accomplishment, improves team performance, and produces above average performance. With learning taking place in the execution process, the organization becomes better at solving its own problems and at making continuous progress. In short, the SCP is implemented in such a way that the organization learns about change and develops the capability to recognize and implement strategic change in the future.

The design and implementation of the SCP is dominated by the transition management practices associated with OD. Beckhard and Pritchard (1992) note that effectively managing a transition requires four activities:

1. Activity planning
2. Commitment planning
3. Communication planning
4. Resource planning

*Activity planning* involves describing the various tasks, both large and small, that need to be carried out in order to move the organization from its current state to its desired state. Activity planning also specifies roles and mechanisms, such as project leaders or special task forces, that will guide implementation activities. *Commitment planning* helps to manage internal political forces and ensures there is a high level of ownership in the change process. *Communication planning* provides managers and employees with the information needed about what is changing, why it is changing, and when change will occur. It helps to manage the uncertainty associated with transitions. Finally, the transition state requires *resource planning* to carry out its activities. Time, people, money, training, and consultants are often needed to see the process through to completion. The transition management activities are clearly aligned with the ISC process. In particular, the design and implementation of the SCP represents the way in which the organization will commit to the transition.

Thus the ISC process borrows from OD's process orientation and strategic management's content orientation to produce a sequence of activities aimed at generating and managing fundamental shifts in strategy and/or organization design. In the next section, we describe a case study of strategic change in which the ISC process was used to produce real and meaningful change in a data processing organization.

## A Case Example

In this final section, we describe the ISC process as it unfolded in a service organization that was part of the savings and loan (S&L) industry.[1]

---

### ISC at On-Line Data Systems

*In 1986, On-Line Data Systems (OLDS) was the largest provider of real-time transaction processing services in the state. Utilizing a potent combination of low-cost hardware and software, OLDS came to dominate the S&L industry, holding well over 50 percent market share with S&Ls accounting for almost 90 percent of its revenues. Originally owned by two other S&Ls, OLDS recently had been "spun off" as a separate and independent business. The reliable provision of low-cost transaction services remained a viable and profitable strategy. Although customer complaints were loud and frequent, OLDS's dominant position in the market allowed managers and employees to respond slowly to these complaints.*

*In 1988, a number of challenges emerged to threaten OLDS's comfortable position. Although profits were good, the firm's chairman and long-time president decided to sell it and take an early retirement. The firm was bought by an entrepreneurial executive who had recently left a major data processing firm. Also at that time, technological, competitive, and economic changes were occurring. The low-cost hardware and software system that had driven costs down was clearly obsolete and started to "crash" more frequently. The system problems caused customer complaints to rise to un-*

---

[1] This case was first described in Cummings and Worley (1993).

*precedented levels. Economically, the S&L industry was beginning to suffer the effects of the recession and of a falling real-estate market. Given OLDS's poor customer service, several larger customers began investigating the possibility of doing their own transaction processing. Finally, the OLDS's culture, a product of industry dominance, formal structures, and low rates of change, was bureaucratic, arrogant, and slow.*

*The new owner quickly announced the need for major changes. Several executives left or were replaced. The manager of the operations department, however, remained. Nearing retirement, he was viewed negatively by younger employees with more technical know-how because of his resistance to change and autocratic management style. He was also viewed unfavorably by the new owner, who had no choice but to rely on his intimate knowledge of the current hardware and software systems.*

*The new owner was concerned that OLDS needed significant changes and so brought in an OD consultant to assist in formulating and implementing them. An extensive strategic analysis of the organization's current strategy and design was conducted. It confirmed that OLDS had relied far too long on a product that was now obsolete. Worse, the primary customer's industry was undergoing important structural changes that threatened OLDS's existence. The current organization had neither the technical expertise nor the managerial skills to carry out a strategic change effort.*

*The OD practitioner suggested a two-day workshop for senior managers in order to review the data and formulate strategic alternatives. The strategy-making process began with a summary statement by the new owner and his expressing of a sense of urgency concerning the need for change. Over the next few hours, participants utilized their own beliefs as well as input from employees that had been gathered during the strategic analysis to develop strategy options for OLDS. One strategy came to be called "Technological Renaissance." It focused on upgrading the hardware and software components of the business. Another strategy, called "Customer Service," targeted the sales and service departments in an effort to improve customer satisfaction. A third strategy, "Market Diversification," suggested that OLDS take its basic service capabilities and address new markets such as insurance firms, banks, securities brokers, and hospital systems. Obviously, combinations were possible. But these three approaches represented the firm's basic strategy choices.*

*As managers discussed the relative merits of the three approaches, the OD consultant observed a lack of attention to organizational issues. He helped the group to see that none of the changes being contemplated could be implemented by the current organization. An old functional structure, formal rules and behaviors, and traditional jobs—all signaled considerable resistance to any change initiative. It became clear to participants that the most important element of an SCP would need to be a human resources development project. At the workshop's conclusion, each participant was asked to assess the different strategic choices in preparation for another meeting.*

*At the next meeting, the following decisions were made as part of the firm's SCP. First, despite the importance of the organizational issues, the greatest threat to the long-term health of OLDS was the market. Therefore the market diversification strategy would be pursued as a long-term initiative. A task force of senior managers was formed to research potential markets and to recommend those most likely to provide a stable source of growth for OLDS over the next three to five years. Second, the technological renaissance and customer focus strategies were postponed. Instead, the managers committed to a six-month period of human resource development. They reasoned that any technical renaissance would place pressure on organizational structure, communication, and short-term performance. The current skills and attitudes of organizational members would not support such change. Similarly, establishing a customer service orientation without the technological base to support it seemed shortsighted. Based on their vision of adopting and implementing state-of-the-art computing systems as well as developing a strong service orientation, managers decided that a concerted effort at management and employee development would need to precede adoption of the new strategies.*

*The OD consultant was asked to design a training program for middle- and first-line managers as well as other employees. It was to include skill development in leadership, teamwork, conflict management, and managing lateral relations. The trainees were to be told of management's commitment to customer service and technological upgrading. They were to be polled systematically on potential technologies and customer service strategies. In addition, they were to be educated about the activities of the task force on market diversification.*

*Over the next six months, managers and employees learned new skills and participated in the development of a technological change plan. They identified likely new technologies that could support the organization's strengths and maintain its share of the S&L market. In addition, customers were surveyed and training programs were developed to support a new customer-focused culture. The high levels of participation produced strong commitment to the new strategies.*

*In 1990, the firm announced the adoption of a new technical system and sought to implement it rapidly. Customer service training was also initiated and included bringing customers to OLDS to view the implementation of the new hardware and software system. In addition, customers were*

*offered training on the new system in order to smooth the transition to it.*
*Despite the S&L industry's restructuring and the Resolution Trust*
*Corporation's takeover of several customers, OLDS maintained its share of*
*the S&L market. In late 1990, OLDS announced the signing of its first ser-*
*vice contract to the insurance industry and estimated that this new market*
*would account for over 25 percent of revenues within three years.*

## Summary

In this chapter, we offered a process model of integrated strategic
change and demonstrated it through a short case about a data processing firm. The ISC model reflects the primary elements of a strategic change definition. First, strategic change is caused by major shifts
in a firm's industry or environment. Second, the content and process
of strategic change are described by a model that analyzes the firm's
strategic orientation, visions and specifies a desired strategic orientation, and then builds an SCP to bring the new strategic orientation
into existence. Finally, such a process is expected to result in improved organizational performance and effectiveness.

In the following chapters, we explain the ISC model in more
detail and demonstrate through the use of short cases and examples
how the model has been applied in organizations.

# 3

# Performing A Strategic Analysis: The VIP Process

The first step in the ISC process is strategic analysis. It is a diagnostic step that brings a senior management team and other key stakeholders together

1. to assess the organization's readiness for strategic change and management's willingness to support and carry out such change,
2. to identify the key values, internal and external issues, and organizational priorities that need to be addressed or accounted for, and
3. to examine the firm's current strategic orientation ($S_1/O_1$).

In this chapter, we describe the first two activities. The third activity, diagnosing the current strategic orientation, is described in Chapter 4. How the strategic analysis step fits in with the other parts of the ISC process is shown in Figure 3.1.

This chapter is divided into three major sections. The first is an overview of the activities in the strategic analysis step. The second describes the process of diagnosing management's readiness for change. The final section is devoted to the VIP Process.

## Activities Performed During Strategic Analysis

The activities of strategic analysis are shown in Figure 3.2 (on page 28) and provide the input for Step 2, strategy making. Although each of the activities are discussed separately, each is dependent on the others, and should be viewed as an integrated whole.

The first activity in strategic analysis is assessing senior management's readiness and ability to carry out strategic change. Senior

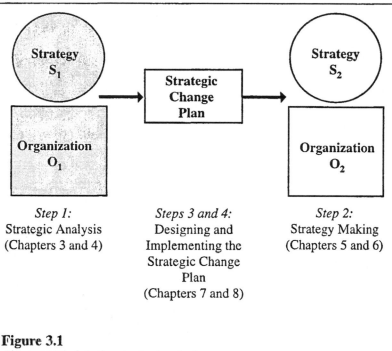

**Figure 3.1**
*The ISC Model: Strategic Analysis*

managers have primary responsibility for overseeing the strategic analysis process. Although there are many reasons for failed strategic change, lack of support for the effort or lack of skills and knowledge associated with formulating and implementing change are certainly among those at the top of the list. Proceeding without a clear sense of senior management's willingness and ability to implement change is a sign of trouble.

The second activity is the VIP Process, an acronym that describes the primary content issues associated with the process. These issues are clarifying the organizational *values and assumptions,* identifying the relevant internal and external strategic *issues,* and *prioritizing* diagnostic and change activities. The VIP Process thus initiates strategic change and builds the foundation for strategic analysis. It sets the scope, boundaries, resources, and urgency of the next activity.

The third activity, diagnosing the organization's current strategic orientation ($S_1/O_1$), determines the reasons for current performance

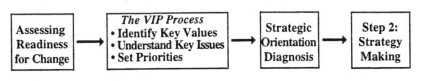

**Figure 3.2**
*Activities in the Strategic Analysis Process*

and effectiveness, the fit between the firm's strategy and organization, and the firm's capabilities.

Strategic analysis activities consist of several popular strategic management techniques that are enhanced by the OD Perspective and several OD techniques applied to strategic management processes. First, assessing readiness for change is a standard OD process that recognizes that change is not likely to occur unless organization members see that change will probably relieve current pressures or problems. Second, the VIP Process brings together many OD and strategic management techniques and processes. Included in the VIP Process, for example, is the assessment of key internal and external issues. To understand these issues, we describe how traditional SWOT (the acronym for strengths, weaknesses, opportunities, and threats) techniques can be enhanced by increased levels of participation. Such involvement is typically missing in most strategic management processes. Third, the diagnosis of the firm's strategic orientation is guided by models and processes from both OD and strategic management. For example, OD relies heavily on diagnostic processes that isolate the causes of current performance and identify the strategic levers for change. Both strategy and OD rely on frameworks, models, and techniques to assess an organization's strategic orientation.

## Diagnosing Management's Readiness for Change

The initial activity in strategic analysis is to convene the senior management team and assess its readiness and ability to successfully carry out strategic change. Both of these conditions are important. First, there must be a readiness to change. This includes a recognition that change is both desirable and necessary because either performance is declining, an important change in competitive conditions is occurring or about to occur, or there is some indication of other organizational problems. If there is no felt need for change, then there is little chance that any substantive strategic change will occur. Second, there must be an ability to carry out change. If senior management does not have the necessary skills and knowledge, attempting strategic change is likely to produce sub-optimal results, increase cynicism in the organization, and lower the organization's capacity for change in the future. Our series of examples following two organizations through the ISC process begins with the following Legal Publishing Company case. This case shows how troublesome team dynamics can impede the advancement of strategy formulation.

---

### Legal Publishing Company: Assessing Readiness for Change

*The executive committee of the Legal Publishing Company (LPC), a producer of legal interpretations, had made several important decisions regarding their strategy and organization over the past several years. These decisions included pursuing new electronic formats for their products and restructuring operations. As a result of these changes, many new members had been hired with specific skills and knowledge believed necessary if LPC was to implement its strategy. Unfortunately, while these people had the technical skills and knowledge in specific areas, they had, for the most part, little knowledge or experience in the legal publishing business. The president of LPC decided that the time was right to call the executive committee together to begin discussions on how to leverage their new skills and abilities into more specific strategies and tactics. She put her senior VP of market strategy in charge of the three-day retreat and offered him the consulting resources that had helped the organization to formulate and implement the strategic and structural changes over the previous year.*

*The SVP, with the consultant's help, designed a workshop to help educate the group on strategy and strategic planning issues, including work around defining current and future products, understanding and defining the markets served, and gaining clarity around who the customer should be. Very early into the first day of the workshop, the group began to display some rather dysfunctional behaviors:*

- *Their discussions rarely reached closure.*
- *Their interchanges were more indirect than direct; that is, they talked about each other rather than to each other.*
- *Their interchanges could be characterized by, "Well, that's very interesting, but I can say what you just said better" and by arguing just for the sake of arguing.*

- *The discussions rarely stayed on point; they strayed wildly from the original topic.*

*It soon became clear to the consultant that further attempts at discussing strategy content would have to be delayed until the team resolved several issues. Among the more salient of these were the assimilation of new members into the group, the president's relationships with the group, and the development of decision-making and conflict-resolution processes. These issues came to be known as the "600 pound gorilla." Until the group dealt with the issues that made up the gorilla, there was no way they could cogently discuss the content issues of strategy. Thus, while the time may have been right to advance their strategies, their inability to discuss content issues in an integrated fashion evidenced their lack of cohesiveness and readiness for change.*

---

For these reasons, senior management teams may need to engage in team-building activities that establish clear goals for the strategic change effort, clear roles and responsibilities, decision-making procedures, norms of conduct, and other isues.

In addition to establishing processes that help to form a more integrated team, senior management must get a handle on the dynamics that might help or hinder strategic change. That is, designing strategic change processes can quickly become politicized if the relationships between the CEO or team leader and his/her direct reports are not understood. Larry Greiner (1986) has developed a matrix that can help to shed light on the political dynamics within a top management team (Figure 3.3). One dimension concerns the willingness of the CEO or organizational leader to exercise power and authority, while the other reflects the willingness of key subordinates to accept the leader's influence.

Depending on the circumstances, a top management team can find itself making decisions in one of four ways. First, when the CEO is willing to exert influence and the key subordinates are willing to accept the CEO's lead, active consensus exists. There is give and take around strategic business issues, decisions get made, and commitment to take action exists.

In the other quadrants, one or both of these dimensions is out of alignment and a less than ideal context for formulating and implementing strategic change exists. In a second way in which decisions can be made, the CEO's influence is high but the subordinates' willingness to join with the CEO is low. Hence, there is covert resistance.

Willingness of the CEO to Exert Influence

| | | Low | High |
|---|---|---|---|
| Willingness of Subordinates to Follow | **High** | Passive Loyalty | Active Consensus |
| | **Low** | Peer Rivalry | Covert Resistance |

**Figure 3.3**
*Top Management Team Political Dynamics*

From Greiner and Schein, POWER AND ORGANIZATION DEVELOPMENT, ©1988 Addison-Wesley Publishing Co., Reading, MA. Reprinted with permission.

In this case, it will be difficult for the CEO to initiate and follow through with strategic change because pockets of resistance exist in key positions. Third, when the CEO is unwilling to lead a group of willing subordinates, a condition of passive loyalty exists. Under these conditions, there is a vacuum of leadership and any latent demand for change is likely to lie dormant. It is possible for a strong subordinate to initiate change, but that person's effectiveness may be limited by the CEO's low level of support. Fourth, strategic change is least likely to occur in any coordinated way if the CEO is unwilling to exert influence and key subordinates are unwilling to accept direction. Peer rivalry suggests that each individual manager is pursuing his/her own self interest and the necessary critical mass of resources is not likely to exist.

If any condition other than active consensus characterizes top management team dynamics, then the best first step in strategic change is to engage in team-building efforts beyond that described above. Proceeding with strategic change without consensus is likely to produce commitments to the status quo. While that may not be a problem if little change is appropriate, it becomes an issue if more substantive change is necessary. Under passive loyalty, the CEO's unwillingness to lead means subordinate initiatives are not given the attention or resources required. Conversely, covert resistance suggests that CEO initiatives for change will be ignored, sabotaged, or left to wither on the vine. In either case, anything more than a commitment to the status quo is highly unlikely. A more formal application of this readiness for change notion is described in the following case, which introduces the second organization that we will follow.

---

### *Sullivan Hospital System: Readiness for Change*

*At the Sullivan Hospital System (SHS), CEO Donald Fulton expressed concern about market share losses to other local hospitals over the previous six to nine months and about declines in patient satisfaction measures. To him and his senior administrators, the need to revise SHS's strategy was clear. It was also clear that such a strategic change would require the enthusiastic participation of all organization members, including nurses, physicians, and managers. The first meeting of the combined management teams from the two hospitals in the system was a three-day retreat to begin the process of strategic change. The hospitals believed that a TQM process would be appropriate for two primary reasons. First, they believed that improving patient care would give physicians a good reason to use the hospital, thus improving the hospitals' market share. Second, the primary governmental regulatory body, the Joint Commission on Accreditation of Healthcare Organizations (JCAHO), was enacting policies requiring hospitals to adopt TQM principles. The team readily agreed that they lacked adequate skills and knowledge associated with implementing a TQM process. They gathered to hear about the history of TQM and the issues that would need to be addressed if TQM were to be implemented. In addition, several exercises were held to get the team to examine decision-making methods, to learn how teams solve problems using TQM processes, and to explore their understanding of the hospitals' current missions, goals, and strategies.*

*At SHS, the senior team consisted of the top administrative teams from the two hospitals in the system. Donald, CEO of the system and president of the larger of the two hospitals, was joined by Mary Fenton, administrator of the smaller hospital. Their two styles were considerably different. Whereas Donald was calm, confident, and mild-mannered, Mary was assertive, enthusiastic, and energetic. Both wanted this strategic change effort to succeed, but Donald's style was considerably more subdued. Still, he hired a consultant for the management of the strategic change effort and devoted considerable resources to hire a Big Six accounting/consulting firm to oversee some major work redesign efforts. Thus, despite differences in style, both administrators demonstrated willingness to lead the change effort.*

*More easily diagnosed was the willingness of the subordinates to follow. Each was clearly enthusiastic about the change process and was clearly taking whatever initiative Donald and Mary would allow or empower them to do. Thus it was believed that there existed a situation of near "active consensus" with regard to the change project. So the next steps were taken.*

---

## The VIP Process

The second activity in strategic analysis is called the VIP Process. The VIP Process is a quick, initial scan of the organization's *values and basic assumptions;* its key *issues,* or the internal and external strengths, weaknesses, opportunities, and threats; and any pressing *priorities* that need to be addressed. Accomplishing these outcomes is the responsibility of the senior management team and provides important guidelines regarding and constraints on subsequent strategic analysis activities. If diagnosing the firm's strategic orientation occurs without these data, then much time, effort, and resources can be wasted conducting an analysis that is too broadly focused or focused on the wrong issues.

For example, too often in strategic change efforts there is a headlong rush into the traditional elements of strategic planning. Staff groups forecast market trends and managers develop operating budgets. Seen through the lens of the organization's culture, these issues and budgets then serve as the basis for organizational goals, or high-level meetings occur to discuss how capital budgets should be allocated. In these cases, the most salient issues in the industry, or the issues most likely to become salient in the next few years, are not addressed, or worse, the people who can provide such vital information are ignored. The VIP Process thus proposes that several pieces of information need to be in place and well understood before the formal process begins. While the length and content of the VIP Process varies depending on the sophistication of the organization, we have found it a useful way to initiate strategic change.

### Conducting a VIP Process

A senior management team has two basic choices of how to conduct the VIP Process. If the organization is new to strategic management or does not have a well-developed strategic planning process, then it makes sense to give each step in the process detailed attention. This is because most of the issues probably are not clear or not readily available as strategic information. On the other hand, if the organization is more sophisticated in its strategic processes or if there is a greater sense of urgency, the VIP Process can be conducted relatively quickly. We begin this section with an example of the latter process and then break out the separate functions in greater detail. In the following case, discussions of organizational values, strategic issues, and action priorities are woven together throughout the process and demonstrate well how they can be dealt with relatively seamlessly.

### The VIP Process (Short Version)

A "VIP Workshop" was held for a mid-sized firm that exports agricultural products for several farming cooperatives. In the past, these cooperatives (suppliers to the business) had exported their products directly. Preventing them from returning to this practice was the driving force behind the firm's initiative for a strategic change process.

Data about the organization, including descriptions of its current strategy, the issues it faced, its internal expertise, and current levels of stress, were gathered prior to the workshop through interviews with senior management and most managers. Financial data and projections were also brought to the workshop.

The workshop was attended by twenty senior managers, including key salespeople and the founder. Early discussions focused on the organization's history, clarifying its best successes, turning points, and disappointments. The participants' collective assumptions about the market place and their added value to their suppliers were clarified and made explicit. Fears such as losing control of the business or losing key export markets were also discussed. The founder explained his core values and principles and in the process eliminated several possible courses of action such as issuing stock options and going public.

The group then engaged in an exercise that generated the following list, the "Enemies of Great Strategies." It represented the key values and assumptions that the participants had about the business.

| Strategic Enemy | Value or Assumption |
|---|---|
| Conceptual Ruts | "We must serve all countries to keep our position abroad." |
| Core Assumptions | "This will always be a family-owned company and our managers will not own any part of it." |
| Conventional Wisdom | "Agricultural research will never come up with replacement products." |
| Extrapolation | "Our growth in certain regions will continue at at least last year's level." |
| Imitation | "We can do better in France if we adopt our French competitor's approach to certain market segments." |

| | |
|---|---|
| Denominator Management | *"We can increase our ROI by closing the office in France and cutting head-quarters' staff."* |
| Success Recipes | *"We've always participated in six European Trade shows and brought our largest customers to the show to visit our suppliers."* |

*The group agreed that the strategic enemy assumptions channeled and restricted inventive problem solving.*

*In the next part of the workshop, the group was presented with a list of about twenty critical issues that had surfaced during the pre-workshop interviews. Each participant was asked to assign each issue a priority: high, medium, or low. Totaling everyone's responses led to the clarification and "clustering" of issues. The group then broke into subgroups according to personal interest and expertise in order to tackle five clusters of issues. From the subgroups came nearly forty suggestions for immediate actions to address key issues.*

*To focus attention on the key action items, the group used the firm's recently revised mission statement as the "umbrella objective" against which suggested actions were measured. The facilitator improvised two critical tests for high priority: The actions must either capture a business opportunity that is short lived or directly support or protect a distinctive competence that is central to achieving strategic objectives.*

*As a result of this process, three actions emerged as highest priorities. First, an opportunity to acquire a large competitor emerged. The competitor's parent firm could not accept the shrinking margins of the business and was looking to sell. Second, managers wanted to explore the possibility of customizing contracts with each supplier to better meet their own objectives (prior to this, all contracts were identical). Third, the exhausting global travel schedule of key personnel (who were now viewed as critical resources to retaining the firm's distinctive competence of selling abroad) needed to be changed.*

*Action programs were formulated to address these three priorities. Immediate actions were scheduled to pursue the acquisition, legal research was started on the customized contracting, and a personnel crisis team was appointed to work on improving work/life balance and restructuring job assignments and work processes to reduce heavy travel for certain key staff members.*

*One year later, the acquisition of the competitor involving a consortium of suppliers was complete. Customized contracting was being piloted, and early signs were that the firm had pioneered a new industry practice that was becoming the wave of the future. And heavy foreign travel had been shifted to young, single professionals, thereby significantly increasing their authority and responsibility and reducing the amount of travel by senior managers who had families and who were nearing burnout.*

*The success of these three priority actions demonstrate the tangible value of the VIP workshop. Perhaps of equal value was the team building, trust building, and opening up of the management team. Frank debate became the norm, and phrases from the workshop such as "stepping out of the box with your thinking" and "middle-laning" (striving for a better work/life balance) have become a common part of this firm's dialogue and culture.*

---

In the long version of the VIP Process, specific attention is given to each element and task forces or focused workshops are convened to address each issue directly. This is an especially appropriate process for organizations new to the strategic change process or for those whose management believes some detailed work is required on the values, issues, or priorities.

***External and Internal Issues.*** An important objective of the VIP Process is to identify the critical strategic issues the organization faces. The idea is not to solve or address those issues, but simply to get senior management and other stakeholders to brainstorm internal and external problems and opportunities. Doing this serves to develop a common frame of reference and narrow the range of issues on which further analysis can take place.

A SWOT analysis is one of the most popular tools within strategic management. It addresses the internal *strengths* and *weaknesses* of the organization as well as its external *opportunities* and *threats*. The SWOT analysis, in combination with the OD Perspective, is a very powerful tool.

Traditionally, a SWOT analysis is carried out exclusively by senior management teams, with some input from specialized staff groups. While it often produces powerful results, it also suffers from many of the problems associated with change efforts that do not involve people in the decisions that affect them; namely, lack of support and little innovation.

In the following example, Withers-Messall, a subsidiary of the Legal Publishing Company, successfully modified the SWOT methodology to generate a rich and diverse set of perspectives on its business.

---

### Withers-Messall: Identifying External and Internal Issues

*At Withers-Messall (WM), the California-based subsidiary of LPC, technological change was threatening to erode its traditional mission of providing printed material that interpreted and reported the changing legal environment in the state. It also threatened WM's reputation and the market share advantages it had held for years. Legal research, case law, and other interpretations were becoming available on CD-ROM. CD-ROM publishers simply mailed clients a new CD every month rather than adding a paper-based supplement to existing volumes of bound materials, as a traditional publisher did. The technology also made information retrieval much faster, since the CD-ROM format allowed the computer to do the searching instead of a person's having to leaf through hundreds of pages of material.*

*WM's executive team recognized they possessed limited knowledge concerning competitor moves, client wants and needs, and operational/production requirements in relation to the new technology. In an effort to understand the issues and priorities the firm was facing, a "high-involvement SWOT" was convened. In essence, customers, field sales representatives, editors, production managers, and internal technology experts were invited to a two-day workshop to identify the opportunities and threats that were specifically represented by the new technology.*

*In preparation for the workshop, participants were asked to think about the firm's competitors, to collect articles concerning CD-ROM, and to look for trends and events that might impact WM. During the first day, participants were divided into small groups and put through a series of tasks. First, they were asked to describe the articles or trends they had collected or noticed and discuss why they thought it was an important issue for WM to address. They then listed and prioritized the issues (opportunities and threats) and reported back to the larger group. The lists from all groups were then combined and prioritized. For the second task, the top opportunities and threats were listed on a large envelope, one per envelope. Each group then received one envelope and was given five minutes to brainstorm answers to the question, "What would happen to WM or its operating environment if this trend were to occur?" After five minutes, the envelopes were rotated and the procedure repeated until each group had brainstormed answers to each issue. When the groups received their original issue, they were given time to examine all of the brainstormed answers and to develop a con-sensus answer about the impact of that trend on WM. In addition, each group answered the question, "What could WM do to address this opportunity or threat?" The results of their discussions were then reported to the larger group.*

*On the second day, the focus turned to internal strengths and weak-nesses. First, each of several groups was assigned to represent a key stake-holder, such as the parent organization (LPC), employees, competitors, or customers. The groups were then asked to address WM's weaknesses by an-swering a question from that stakeholder's perspective. For example, the competitor group addressed the question, "We can attack WM because they are... ." After the groups reported out, the facilitator captured the weak-nesses seen by each group and developed a list of common key weaknesses. To address WM's strengths, the groups were mixed up, but the same process was used, although with different questions. For example, the group repre-senting the competitor's point of view was asked to respond to the question, "What keeps me awake at night is worrying that WM might... ." Again, as the organization's strengths were reported out, a summary list was created.*

*The high-involvement SWOT produced a large volume of high-qual-ity information that quickly revealed the key issues that needed to be ad-dressed, accounted for, or leveraged by the executive team in response to the technological change. It also exposed organizational members to the com-plexity of the problem and built consensus for the need for change.*

---

There are many other excellent approaches to scanning and analyzing a firm's internal and external environment. They all share, however, the goal of conducting a more detailed analysis of either the organization or its environment. However, the purpose at this stage of the ISC process is simply a quick scanning of the key issues the firm faces. A more detailed look at the internal organization is conducted during the analysis of the firm's strategic orientation, which is de-tailed in Chapter 4. If the organization's management believes a more formal analysis of the external environment is warranted, several ex-ternal analysis techniques are available; we list them in Table 3.1. They include industry analysis, competitor analysis, and scenarios.

Each of these techniques has received considerable attention elsewhere and a full discussion of them is beyond the scope of this book. However, each is important because it can benefit from the in-tegration of the OD Perspective. For example, industry analysis is a technique popularized by Michael Porter (1980) to understand the

**Table 3.1**
*Alternative Environmental Scanning Methods*

| Method | Purpose |
| --- | --- |
| Industry attractiveness | To determine the bargaining power of buyers and suppliers, the threat of entry and substitute products, and the rivalry among firms |
| Scenarios | To determine the likely course of industry evolution |
| Competitor analysis | To understand competitor assumptions strategies, goals, and likely actions |

economic attractiveness (profitability) and structure of an industry. An industry is attractive to the extent there are weak buyers and suppliers, there is little threat of entry into the industry or of substitute products/services, and rivalry among firms is low. The technique can accommodate broad participation that not only improves the richness of the data considered but also builds commitment and ownership of the process of strategic change. For example, sales and marketing groups can provide valuable information about buyers, purchasing departments can provide market intelligence about suppliers, and technical staffs understand threats from substitute products. Thus even the traditional and more content-oriented processes can benefit from the OD Perspective.

*Clarifying Values and Assumptions.* The OD perspective suggests that any organization that undertakes a strategic change effort, whether it has years of strategic management experience or is new to the process, needs to clearly understand its values and assumptions before the formal change process can begin. That is, an effective strategic change process requires knowledge of the constraints and enablers of change. In short, the organization must understand the extent to which its culture will impact strategic change processes.

The ISC process views culture as both an *outcome* of prior choices around strategy and organization and a *foundation* for change that can either facilitate or hinder movement to a new strategic orientation. From the outcome perspective, all organizations are imbued with a **culture**—a set of values and basic assumptions about how to solve problems that works well enough to be taught to others (Schein, 1993). Organizational culture is an emergent phenomenon that is often formed early in an organization's life or in response to critical events and is a direct result of the organization's strategic orientation. Designing and implementing strategic orientations is a difficult managerial task that must balance individual needs, political concerns, and technical demands. As a result, few strategic orientations are perfectly constructed and organization members must find ways to produce goods and services despite the imperfections in strategy and organization design. When these ways work well enough, they are taught to others and become embedded in the informal unconscious of the organization.

From the foundational perspective, these values and assumptions about correct behavior operate at a relatively unconscious level. As a result, there is little chance of anyone's directly intervening to change organization culture. The purpose of values and assumption clarification in the VIP Process is to get a quick but realistic handle on the organization's current culture. Such an effort, we believe, will clearly set out constraints to change or clearly identify the targets of change (although changing culture is a long and difficult process). Successful strategic change will recognize these constraints and either work with them or around them. Organizations that attempt strategic changes that conflict with these values and assumptions must recognize the gravity of their choices and be doubly sure they have the resources, the political clout and support, and the time to engage in such an effort. In short, integrated strategic change is *not* a cultural change process. Over time and with the successful transition in a firm's strategic orientation, cultural change may take place, but it is not the focus of this model.

Again, the purpose of the VIP Process is to quickly scan the organization and its environment. A full analysis of a firm's culture typically requires much more time and effort than can be devoted at this point. This is not to say that a full cultural analysis may not be warranted. For example, two major electric utility firms had announced their intention to merge and so, as part of the due diligence process, engaged a consultant to analyze their cultures in some depth. The analysis showed considerable differences between them. These differences ultimately were an important reason in the decision to call off the merger. More commonly, however, what is required is a relatively direct way of identifying the organization's core identity. A core identity defines why the organization produces certain products/

**Table 3.2**
*Potential Value-Based Identities*

- A product- or service-driven firm
- A customer- or market-driven firm
- A production- or technology-driven firm
- A sales- and marketing-driven firm
- A results-driven firm

---

services, why it relates to markets in certain ways, or why it organizes the way it does.

Table 3.2 lists several potential identities that answer the question, "What kind of a firm are we?"

An organization's values and assumptions can be understood by determining its "driving force" (Robert, 1993). By establishing a debate among its managers about the beliefs that really drive who the organization is and what it does, the organization can better see the constraints and facilitators to change. A description of the values-clarification process at Withers-Messall is described next.

---

### Withers-Messall: Clarifying Organizational Values

*After WM's "high-involvement SWOT" process, its senior management team met to understand the values and assumptions that might help or hinder the strategic change process. The process began by describing and defining each of the basic identities. For example, a customer- or market-driven firm is oriented around satisfying particular users or market segments; satisfying these end users is the firm's primary focus. In a production- or technology-driven firm, the firm's identity is wrapped up in what it can produce or because it can, it should produce certain products or services.*

*Once everyone was clear on how the various types of firms differed, the discussion turned to "What is our identity?" or "What really drives our organization?" The debate was heated. One camp argued that since the parent company (LPC) set sales and profit targets and WM was expected to hit them, they were a results-driven firm. They asked people to think about how all-consuming the process of budget creation was each year and how everything else in the organization came to a dead halt during these months as numbers were crunched, objectives set, and budgets prepared. Another camp argued that the whole organization was built around a production orientation.*

*They reasoned that with the large amount of editorial capability embedded in the organization, WM's whole reason for being was to produce something, anything, that the sales force would get sold. This group asked, "If we could produce a (type of product) really well even if we didn't know whether anyone would buy it, would we produce it?" They suggested that the answer was traditionally, "Yes." A third camp believed the firm was market- and customer-driven. The organization's mission statement clearly stated that it served the legal market and that all of WM's products were oriented toward helping the lawyer understand the substantive and pertinent legal issues of a case. Finally, a fourth camp proposed that WM was a sales- and marketing-driven firm. It had the largest direct sales force in the industry and was known for its aggressive yet high-touch sales efforts.*

*Each argument was compelling and the debate remained intense for hours. During a break, several subgroups continued to argue one side and then another. Eventually, three issues emerged. First, the group came to believe that one of the root causes for its average performance over the previous few years was that all of the arguments were true and that WM had never really established its core identity. Second, the group recognized that the technological threat posed by the CD-ROM had clearly challenged the organization and that* its lack of clarity regarding how to respond was a function of its "multiple personality." *Third, the group looked* at what the organization's identity had been *over the previous fifty years. They saw clearly that the organization was production-driven. WM made products and services* because it could, *whether or not there was demand for those products and services. The organization had found several "creative" ways to push products out the door.*

*Thus WM saw itself as having a strong production and editorial orientation. It also was operating under several values and assumptions, including the beliefs that*

- *its editorial capability was its key to success,*
- *the sales force was a "sacred cow,"*
- *editorial was "first among equals,"*
- *they were meek in their relations with LPC, and*
- *the employees had a strong commitment to the history of WM but not to its current image.*

*Each of these values and assumptions were then discussed as to how they might help or hinder the strategic change process.*

*Prioritizing Action Items.* The final activity in the VIP Process involves gaining consensus on the priority issues, problems, questions, or other activities to be specifically addressed in the analysis of the firm's strategic orientation. The process must strive for consensus among the participants as to which issues and actions demand highest priority. Responsibility for this process typically falls to the top manager (CEO, President, or Division Manager). The selected issues and priorities are examined as a set to ensure they truly represent the critical strategic issues the firm faces and not some group of random elements. By selecting several important areas for action and research and obtaining the commitment to work on them, the organization can ensure a more efficient strategic analysis process. On the other hand, long lists of generic actions with assignments forced on people not present in the workshop doom the process and follow through to failure.

Finally, agreement is reached about the format and schedule for future strategic change activities. If the process is to be continued, it is important to identify the next steps and assign responsibility for them. This usually involves customizing a formalized strategic change process to fit the organization and the people who are driving the activity.

## Summary

In this chapter, we described the VIP Process and other initial activities associated with strategic analysis. In assessing readiness for change, the organization's senior management team is diagnosed for their willingness and ability to carry out an ISC process. Team building that clarifies the roles and expectations of the CEO and others is strongly encouraged. This cohesive group then becomes responsible for conducting the strategic analysis and subsequent steps in strategic change.

The VIP Process involves a quick scanning of the important values and assumptions of the organization—its key internal strengths and weaknesses as well as its key external opportunities and threats. The Process concludes with a prioritization of the issues to be addressed in the analysis of the firm's strategic orientation.

In the next chapter, we describe the activities associated with the diagnosis of the organization's current strategic orientation.

# 4

# Strategic Analysis: Diagnosing Strategic Orientation

In this chapter, we describe the other major activity in strategic analysis—the assessment of the firm's current strategic orientation ($S_1/O_1$). This activity is designed to determine the root causes of current organizational performance and effectiveness. A diagnostic model is used to assist in the assessment. It views organizational performance in terms of the extent to which a strategic orientation has been well formulated and implemented.

This chapter is divided into two major sections. In the first, we present a framework that represents how strategic content and implementation interact to produce firm performance. In the second, we describe the content areas for diagnosis of the firm's strategic orientation and support them with case examples.

## Causes of Firm Performance

There are two primary determinants of organizational performance: an industry's attractiveness and the organization's strategic orientation. Attractiveness refers to the industry's structure (see Chapter 3) and the extent to which organizations in that industry are protected from new entrants, powerful buyers and suppliers, and rivalry (Porter, 1980). In the short run, industry attractiveness is relatively fixed. This is important to recognize when we speak of superior or above average performance, since we are taking the industry's average performance as the baseline. In this chapter, the focus is on the source of performance that is more amenable to management influence: the firm's strategic orientation. From this perspective, performance derives from the quality of the strategy formulated and the extent to which it is implemented well (Bonoma, 1985). Figure 4.1

suggests that success results from good strategies implemented well and failure from poor strategies implemented poorly. However, organizations play roulette when they attempt to take bad strategies and implement them well, while trouble occurs when a good strategy is implemented poorly.

Failure to achieve strategic objectives, therefore, is not necessarily an indication that the strategy was wrong or that management has failed. In some cases, an organization that fails to meet strategic objectives performs better than could be reasonably expected, considering the poor strategies chosen or the lack of focused organizational resources. In fact, objectives may have been missed by even more were it not for excellent effort or outstanding management. Any number of factors can contribute to both substandard and superior performance. Hence, understanding the reasons for performance, rather than launching into an approach based on untested assumptions, is an important objective of strategic analysis.

Whether the real problem is the strategy or its execution, any new strategy should reflect the organizational learning that results from a thorough diagnosis. A strategic analysis that does not address key organizational issues—such as how work is accomplished, how the organization is structured, or the extent to which control systems collect relevant information—increases the risk of selecting objectives during the strategy making step that are unachievable regardless of the strategy or the efforts to achieve them. Financial information

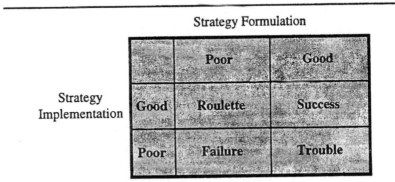

**Figure 4.1**
*Outcomes of Strategy Formulation and Implementation*

alone is not necessarily the best or most reliable indicator of organizational health or the effectiveness of management, for it may lead to erroneous conclusions about the firm's ability to achieve specific objectives. As a result, strategic analysis gives equal attention to external, strategic issues and to the internal capabilities of the present organization.

## Diagnosing a Firm's Strategic Orientation

Figure 4.2 presents in more detail the components of a strategic orientation and their interrelationships.

Our experience with conventional strategic management approaches is that too heavy an emphasis is placed on analyzing the organization's strategy per se. That is, its mission, product positioning, and "strategic intent" receive more attention than do its internal organization, which supports the strategy. Little or no attention is given

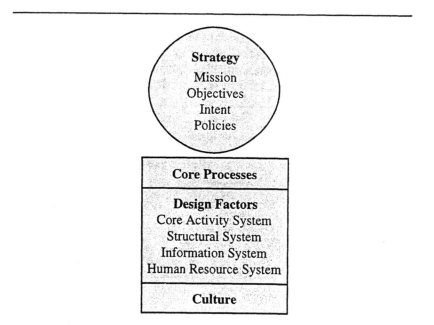

**Figure 4.2**
*Components of Strategic Orientation*

to the *actual capabilities* of the organization to perform. In contrast, the strategic analysis step of the ISC process reflects different priorities and values. While conventional tools of strategy analysis are utilized, it also includes an in-depth assessment of the "reality" of the organization. The assessment looks at the core processes and resources that can be leveraged; the extent to which the organization is designed to support strategic objectives and the core processes; levels of collaboration within and between organizational units; and the overall alignment of the organization with respect to its strategy and structure.

In short, the analysis of the firm's strategic orientation places as much emphasis on understanding the organizational and human constraints and capabilities as it does on understanding and interpreting new product development goals, market share, and financial objectives. A result of this thorough organizational analysis is an increased understanding of the real capabilities and individual commitments toward prescribed strategic changes. The key benefit of such an approach is that the resulting SCP will be more realistic, have a higher level of support and commitment, and an increased chance of being successfully implemented.

### Assessing the Quality of Strategy Formulation ($S_1$)

The first step in determining how well the strategy has been formulated is to ask the following four questions:

1. Other than making a profit, what is the primary purpose of this organization? Why is the firm in business?
2. What are the organization's key financial and operational goals and objectives?
3. How does the organization achieve those objectives? In what ways does it compete?
4. What are the key policies that guide decision making and operation?

These four questions, which are briefly defined in Table 4.1, provide information about the firm's mission, goals and objectives, strategic intent, and functional policies. The second step assesses how well these different elements are aligned with one another, and the final step determines the extent to which the strategy itself addresses environmental demands. The assessment process used to understand the fitness of the Sullivan Hospital System strategy is used to demonstrate the process.

**Table 4.1**
*Elements of a Firm's Strategy*

| Element | Definition |
| --- | --- |
| Mission | A statement that describes the long-term purpose of the organization; the products/services offered and the markets served; the character, image, and range of business interests; and the needs satisfied by the firm's existence. |
| Goals and Objectives | Statements that provide explicit direction; set organizational priorities; provide *the* guidelines for management decisions; and serve as the cornerstones for organizing activities, designing jobs, and standards of achievement. |
| Strategic Intent | A succinct label that describes *how* the organization intends to achieve its goals and objectives. |
| Functional Policies | The organizational methods, procedures, rules, and administrative practices associated with converting plans into results. |

---

### Sullivan Hospital System: Assessing Strategy

*The initial assessment of strategy at SHS included interviews with senior managers from both hospitals as well as a sampling of middle managers and staff (for example, nurses, ancillary professionals, and environmental services providers). Of all the questions, the one pertaining to the mission of the hospitals garnered the most consensus and passion. There was almost unanimous commitment to the* breadth of services *provided and the* values *that played a prominent role in the delivery of those services by a health care organization sponsored by a religious order, such as SHS. A mission and values statement was clearly posted throughout the hospital and many of the items in that statement were repeated almost verbatim in the interviews.*

*From there, however, the answers became more diverse. With respect to goals and objectives, different stakeholder groups saw them differently. Senior administrators were fairly clear about the goals listed in the strategic plan. These goals included increasing measurements of patient satisfaction, decreasing the amount of overtime, and increasing market share.*

*However, below that level there was little awareness of hospital goals or how people influenced their accomplishment.*

*On the question of strategic intent, or how the goals were being achieved, there was a clear split in people's perceptions. Some believed the hospital achieved its objectives through its designation as the area's primary trauma center. They noted that if someone's life were in danger, the best chance of survival was to go to SHS. The problem, respondents joked, was that "after we save their life, we tend to forget about them." Many, however, held beliefs that could be labeled "low cost." That is, objectives were achieved by squeezing out every penny of cost no matter how doing that impacted patient care.*

*Finally, with respect to policies, there was a general belief that the organization was too centralized. People felt little empowerment to make decisions. There also were a number of financial policies that were seen as dictated from the corporate office, where "shared services" existed, including finance, marketing, information systems, and purchasing. Further, several policies limited managers' ability to spend money, especially if it wasn't allocated in budgets.*

---

**Assessing the Alignment Between Strategy Elements.** The starting place for strategy development is the firm's mission. SHS's strategy formulation scored very well here. The mission statement clearly set out the organization's values and therefore described the desired character of the organization. It also stated that the organization's purpose was healing. Although the values and purpose were not specifically stated, they were clearly understood by everyone in the hospital to mean that SHS would provide a broad range of services and would treat anyone who came into the hospital regardless of their ability to pay. Thus both services offered and markets served were broadly defined.

Within the context of this broad purpose, however, SHS's *goals and objectives* were very clear to some but unclear to others. Hofer and Schendel (1978) suggest that the quality of an organization's goals and objectives can be determined by comparing them against the following criteria. Good goals establish the following:

- goal or attribute sought (that is, profits, growth, customer satisfaction, market share),
- an index for measuring progress,

- a target or hurdle to be achieved,
- and a deadline or time frame for accomplishment.

For the senior management team, the goals contained in the strategic plan clearly met these criteria. Specific areas of achievement had been laid out, measures for assessment defined, and time frames articulated. For the rest of the organization, however, these goals were not well understood. This misunderstanding led to some alignment problems, which we discuss next.

When conducting the assessment of strategy, it is important to compare the level of expected or stated goal performance against that of current performance. The gaps between the two levels provide a great deal of information about how well the organization has formulated its strategy. If there are no goals, then one important indicator of formulation effectiveness is lacking and a concerted effort to understand the lack of goals is in order. Goals are as important as a mission statement in terms of their ability to give direction. An organization without goals is likely to have no intentional strategy at all. The gaps between actual and expected performance levels also provide clues about strengths and weaknesses in the organization's strategic planning efforts. Small gaps indicate either that the organization has chosen proper strategies or that the wrong goals were chosen, given the industry's structure. Large gaps indicate either that poor strategies were chosen or that the wrong goals were pursued. Distinguishing between these possibilities requires insight into and judgment regarding the fit between the industry's performance, the organization's desired strategies, its realized strategies, and its goals. In general, though, the larger the gap between desired and current performance, the higher the sense of urgency and readiness for change.

The most integrative concept among the four elements is the organization's *strategic intent*. Strategic intent characterizes the organization's "grand" strategy—the *way* it has attempted to meet its objectives. SHS's situation demonstrates a common problem. Many organizations have failed to make clear choices regarding how to achieve their objectives. Michael Porter (1980) refers to these organizations as "stuck in the middle." In Porter's language, SHS had not clearly chosen between a differentiation strategy or low-cost strategy. A differentiation strategy would have been indicated by the firm's clear attempt to leverage its status in the community as a trauma center, to build "centers of excellence" in certain clinical areas, or to focus on patient-centered care models that put the patient or physician in the spotlight and catered to their needs. A low-cost strategy would have been indicated by a well-developed sense of respect for the importance of keeping costs low. Instead, there was considerable disdain for the cost-cutting and other measures that appeared to hurt patient care.

If strategy has been well formulated, then all organization members are clear about how the organization is trying to achieve its objectives. Notice that we see the clarity and agreement of strategic intent as a formulation issue, not an implementation issue. Actual implementation cannot begin to be successful if no one knows what the strategy is.

In general, strategic intent usually can be conveyed in a simple label that provides an orienting framework for determining the fit of the various pieces of strategy. Table 4.2 (on the next page) lists several of these labels, the goals typically associated with each strategy, and the way the strategy achieves those goals. If data collection efforts do not suggest a clear strategic intent, then an important source of poor performance may be indicated.

Thus, despite the strength of SHS's mission statement, the quality of its strategy formulation efforts was showing signs of weakness. Without a clearly understood strategic intent, the various goals seemed unrationalized. For example, the broad product line and market share goals satisfied those who believed that low cost was the strategy. But it confused and angered those who felt high-quality patient care was the primary intent.

The final element of strategy that must be examined in this first step is the organization's functional policies. A **functional policy** is the organizational methods, procedures, rules, and administrative practices associated with converting strategic intent into results. As guidelines for decision making, policies are not always written down and so often have to be inferred from practice. At SHS, there was good agreement that policies were relatively centralized and tightly controlled. The decision making and financial policies that reflected this philosophy fit well with the low-cost intent, but again, probably frustrated those who believed patient care was the primary driving force.

***Does the Strategy Fit the Industry Environment?*** In the final step, the strategy is examined for its overall "fitness" with environmental demands. The inputs to this assessment are the environmental scanning results (for example, opportunities and threats, industry

**Table 4.2**
*Strategic Intent, Goals, and Means*

| Strategic Intent | Primary Goals | Achieves Goals By... |
|---|---|---|
| Low cost | High market share<br>High sales | Focusing attention and resources on achieving the lowest costs in all segments of the business |
| Differentiation | Profitability | Offering a specialized product/service that is viewed as unique and therefore worth paying more for |
| Focus | Profitability | Dedicating organizational attention and resources to satisfying specific market segments |
| Harvest | Cash flow<br>Profitability | Severely cutting costs to increase margins on products/services that have limited long-term viability |
| Growth | Sales growth above industry average<br>Market share increases | Investing capital expense of current profitability to build a strong position for the future |
| Diversification | Growth in sales | Entering new markets with existing products, extending a product line, or entering whole new businesses |
| Vertical integration | Reduce variation in costs<br>Capture margins from other businesses | Controlling sources of supply (backward integration) or channels of distribution (forward integration) |
| Turnaround | Survival | Taking drastic actions to enhance revenues or cut costs to save the organization |

structure) from the VIP Process and the data from the four questions posed earlier in this chapter. The organization then asks, "Does our current strategy meet the needs and requirements for success in this industry?" At SHS, the data from the four questions were fed back to the senior management team. It generated considerable discussion and eventually a consensus that the organization's current strategy did not fit the needs of the environment. There was ample evidence to explain the decline in market share, patient and physician satisfaction, and morale within the hospital. With respect to the environment, the firm's primary stakeholders (patients and physicians) were "voting with their feet" through admissions to other hospitals. Other stakeholders (corporate office, employees) were also dissatisfied with the current state. Third, with declining volume, unit costs were bound to increase, thereby making it difficult to be profitable or bid competitively for insurance plans. Improvements were clearly needed.

*Summary.* The ISC strategy assessment process (data collection, data feedback, and collective interpretation) clearly reflects the values inherent in the OD Perspective in addition to describing the content of an organization's current strategy. While not all elements may require extensive examination, each contributes an important answer to the questions of why, where, when, how, and on what basis a firm is competing. In the next section, we examine the extent to which the strategy is well implemented. Clearly, linking the elements of strategy with the current organization design provides additional important information in understanding firm performance.

### Assessing the Quality of Strategy Implementation ($O_1$)

The second half of the process of analyzing the firm's strategic orientation consists of determining how well the formulated strategy has been implemented. The criteria for "well implemented" has three parts:

1. Does the current organization support the current strategy (for example, its mission, goals, intent, and policies)?
2. Do the organization's structures and processes focus attention and resources on the things that guarantee the firm's success and survival?
3. Do the individual organization design factors (structure, work design, and human resource systems) support each other?

By examining these different alignments as indicators of implementation, the firm can assure that any potential strategies considered in the strategy making step are viewed realistically in light of organizational capabilities and the resources that will be required to implement them.

We believe the most fruitful way to begin this analysis is to understand the processes most important to the organization's success and survival: its core transformation processes. *These processes represent the key linkage or integrating concept between the elements of strategy and organization.*

***Mapping an Organization's Core Processes.*** Socio-technical systems theory, TQM, and process re-engineering models have provided an important set of tools for understanding how organizations add value. These models can be used to understand how an organization currently delivers products or services.

All organizations can be conceived in terms of the primary processes used to deliver products or services. A **process** is a series of activities or steps that transform inputs into valued outputs. Processes can also be defined as **routines**—regular and predictable patterns of activity that are made up of coordinated actions by individuals. A process map simply lists the different activities used to deliver an organization's products or services. One example is the Value Chain, popularized by Michael Porter (1985) and shown in Figure 4.3. The Value Chain divides the organization into support activities and primary activities. Support activities include human resource systems, technology development, and infrastructure systems (planning, information, legal). Primary activities are represented by inbound logistics (procurement, receiving), operations, outbound logistics (shipping, inventory, distribution), sales and marketing, and service. The Value Chain is a generic map that attempts to describe the elements of most organizations. In the example that follows, the Westin Short Community Hospital used the Value Chain in its strategic analysis.

---

### Understanding the Current Organization at Westin Short Community Hospital

*The Westin Short Community Hospital (WSCH) is located in the southern region of the United States. The Clinton Health Care Reform initiatives, spiraling health care costs, overcapacity in beds brought about by the tremendous growth in health care during the 1960s, and a large, well-endowed competitor at the other end of town—all resulted in a rather tricky and com-*

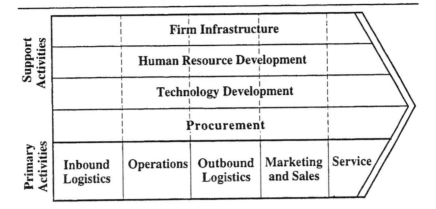

**Figure 4.3**
*Porter's Value Chain*

*plex environment. In-patient projections by the hospital's CFO suggested that WSCH should view itself not as a 300-bed hospital, but as a 100-bed hospital. As part of its strategic analysis process, the hospital sought to understand its current organization. As the first step, it formed a cross-functional task force of managers, employees, and executives to identify the core processes and to begin mapping out the routines within each process.*

*A steering committee that was overseeing the strategic change gave the task force the following four core processes to begin working on:*

1. *Patient services, including treatment, diagnosis, dietary, and other services*
2. *Planning and development, including physician relations, pay or relations, and contracting*
3. *Information and education, including medical records, information systems, and educational services*
4. *Managing the business, including human resource management, facilities planning, and finance*

*Deciding on these four processes was not as easy as it may sound. Organizations often have trouble seeing the "forest for the trees" and incorrectly assume their organization performs dozens of "core" processes. WSCH was no exception, and the steering committee's early meetings were characterized by a pronounced tendency to discuss the details of a service or a department's functions. The consultant intervened often to keep the group focused at an appropriately high level of analysis. Fortunately, the group quickly learned to monitor itself and so began to enjoy the insights that came from their discussions.*

*In the second step, the task force wrestled with the framework given to them and eventually made some modifications, with the steering committee's concurrence. They too believed there were four processes. But they saw the set of core processes as providing patient services, providing physician services, developing relationships with external stakeholders, and managing the business. This evolution in labels is common. The first attempt is often guided by old paradigms of traditional organizations that view things in functional terms or outcomes, rather than as processes. Once that constraint is lifted, the members of the task force "see the light" and become even more involved in the process.*

*This was especially true for the WSCH task force. As they discussed the old "patient services" process (consisting of treatments, diagnosis, dietary, and other services), they believed that breaking down the process by the type of patient would be most helpful. With the consultant's help, they saw that some of the core processes given to them by the steering committee were not processes per se, but rather services, products, or functions. Immediately, they saw that same orientation reflected in their choice of second-level processes, so they abandoned their agenda. With these new insights, the task force took less than an hour to change the names of the four core processes and map the second-level processes associated with providing patient services. A copy of their "Providing Patient Services" core process and its associated second-level processes are shown in Figure 4.4.*

*The generic sequence of inbound logistics, operations, outbound logistics, and sales and marketing in Porter's model can be seen in Figure 4.4. For example, inbound logistics in a hospital takes the form of admitting the patient. Operations takes the form of assessing the patient; performing different procedures such as surgery or ordering a special diet; and restoring the patient. Outbound logistics is represented by patient discharge processes.*

*Once the task force got agreement on the second-level processes for all the core processes, they shared their model with other managers, staff, and executives. They asked for their input on its fundamental accuracy in reflecting how the hospital actually delivered patient care. This involvement took the form of announcing the request for input at a department managers' meeting and then posting the high-level process map (shown in Figure 4.4) in different departments of the hospital. People would look at the map and make a variety of comments on an input form provided. In some cases, they would actually draw on the map itself.*

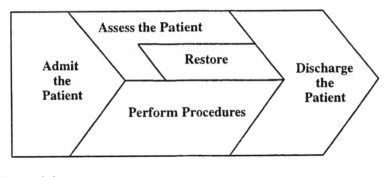

**Figure 4.4**
*The Providing Patient Services Process at Westin Short*

Depending on the organization's needs, two additional steps can be taken. The first involves allocating operating costs to specific second-level processes. Completing this option is particularly insightful because it provides a clear picture of how resources are allocated and can be compared with the firm's strategic intent. But it is not easy because direct cost information is *not* contained in the organization's accounting records according to processes. Accounting information is often classified in terms of cost of goods sold, standard costs for different manufacturing departments, inventory, work in process, and so on. It is not collected in terms of ordering materials, delivering service, or developing new products. As a result, each activity or process needs to be analyzed separately and costs determined and assigned appropriately. The second option involves flow-charting Level III processes. Obviously, an organization can do both.

The advantage of the first option is that the organization can to some degree gain a handle on the extent to which costs line up with strategies (discussed later in this chapter). This would be important for an organization pursuing a cost-based strategy, such as Low Cost, Harvesting, or Defending (see Table 4.2). Allocating a significant proportion of its total operating costs to product development might signal a misfit between strategic intent and strategy implementation. The second option has the advantage that re-engineering an organization often requires this additional level of detail. The cost savings or increased cycle time advantages of re-engineering are facilitated by this information.

*Identifying Dominant/Distinctive Competences.* The next step in assessing the extent to which the strategy has been implemented well is to identify the organization's current dominant and distinctive competences. A **dominant competence** is the set of routines, managerial and technical skills and knowledge, and resources that are most important or salient in determining the organization's ability to survive (McKelvey, 1981). A **distinctive competence** is the unique combination of routines that distinguish a firm from its competitors, the output of which is valued by customers. The distinctive competence is something the organization does particularly well. In many cases, the dominant and distinctive competences are the same, but they need not be. For example, at Club Med the dominant and distinctive competences are in operating vacation villages. Not only must it do this well in order to survive, it is something they do better than any other resort organization, and it is highly valued by customers. On the other hand, the dominant competence of most banks involves ensuring the amount of interest paid to depositors is sufficiently less than the yield the banks receive on their investment portfolios. The routines most valued by customers, though, are often attentive and accurate service features. Identifying either competence, however, begins by examining the high-level process map.

---

### Identifying Dominant and Distinctive Competences at Westin Short

*The task force that had developed the high-level process maps met again to discuss the hospital's dominant and distinctive competences. After discussing the meanings of and differences between the two, the task force began to debate what were the competences of WSCH. It was clear to many members that the dominant competence had something to do with the delivering of patient services. However, the consultant pressed the group to think more deeply. What was it exactly that the hospital had to do to succeed?*

*During this discussion, the task force had an important insight. While they generally agreed that treating patients was a key part of the dominant competence, they were able to see strategically how recent decisions by the competitor hospital had hurt them. WSCH had a strong reputation in the community for being a high-quality (but also high-cost) hospital. That reputation could be seen in the maternity/child delivery program. Many women in the local area specifically asked to have their babies delivered at WSCH. Recently, however, the competitor hospital had purchased a small women's hospital a few blocks from WSCH and had spent a considerable sum upgrading its facilities and image. For the first time, WSCH had some real competition in one of their core businesses. Its high costs quickly became an important weakness.*

*After several discussions among task force members and a number of conversations with the hospital's senior administrators about the hospital's distinctive competence, members' attention soon focused on a high-level process labeled "Providing Physician Services." Many of the administrators argued that the process didn't really exist or was part of another core process such as "Managing the Business." However, the task force convincingly argued that their experience and information clearly indicated that many hospital resources were devoted to the "care and feeding" of the physicians. Further, as the task force looked at their core processes and the customers of those processes, it became clear that the most satisfied customer was the physician. There was a common story within the hospital that although most physicians in the area had privileges at both hospitals, if a physician's spouse was in need of hospitalization, they sent that spouse to WSCH. Thus a consensus emerged that the routine WSCH performed better than any other organization was its delivery of physician services.*

---

In general, identifying the firm's dominant competence is easier than identifying its distinctive competence. Organizations are usually quite aware of what they must do to survive and succeed. However, they are generally unaware of what they do that is valued by the customer. This explains why senior managers often find the exercise of interviewing customers so powerful. For many of them, it is the first time they have ever actually talked to a customer and heard about how they use the firm's outputs. For example, Jack Welch of GE was astounded to learn from customers about GE's inflexibility regarding product offerings, service orientation, and the like. As a result of what he learned, he began encouraging all of his managers to speak regularly with customers.

*Alignment Among Strategy, Core Processes, and Organization Design Factors.* The final and most important step in understanding how well a strategy has been implemented is to examine the alignment among the firm's strategy (its mission, goals, intent, and policies), its core processes (dominant and distinctive competences), and the organization design factors. Design factors include the structural system, core activity systems, information and control systems, and human resource systems (Table 4.3 on the next page).

**Table 4.3**
*Traditional Elements of Organization Design*

| Design Factor | Definition and Issues |
|---|---|
| Structural System | Organization structures tend to distribute along a continuum ranging from bureaucratic and mechanistic to organic and innovative. Mechanistic structures tend to be formal, centralized, have clear lines of authority, and are differentiated. Organic structures tend to be informal, decentralized, and flexible. |
| Core Activity System | The way work is designed to support the dominant and distinctive competences can be based on individual jobs or teams and can vary in terms of the authority given to them to make decisions. |
| Information/ Control Systems | The extent to which information flows facilitate conduct of competences and promote knowledge of strategic objectives |
| Human Resource Systems | The extent to which selection, training, performance appraisal, and reward processes support strategy implementation |

A *structural system* is the basic organizational form chosen to focus attention, resources, and power in the organization. Bureaucratic or mechanistic organizations tend to be rigid, centralized, and differentiated. Organic organizations tend to be flexible, decentralized, and innovative. A *core activity system* is the work designs and departmental structures that directly support the execution of the firm's dominant and distinctive competences. Depending on the required frequency of performance, the uniqueness of each execution, and the interdependencies between specific operations of a process, different work designs are necessary and different departmental structures are required.

The demands of the external environment are the primary driver of structural systems, while the characteristics of the organization's core processes are the drivers of the core activity systems. For example, mechanistic structures are best suited for stable and certain environments, while low uncertainty, low interdependency technologies favor individual jobs and clear limits to behaviors and authority. Organic structures are better suited to unstable and uncertain environments, but uncertain and interdependent technologies favor team-based activity systems that have broader authority and multi-skilled workers. Unfortunately, these two drivers do not always produce structural systems and activity systems that are naturally compatible. For example, law enforcement organizations must reconcile two very different forces. The work is very high in uncertainty and interdependency, which would suggest team-based work designs with decentralized decision making. But the typical law enforcement environment (the city, county and state governments) is very slow moving and stable, which leads to a bureaucratic structure that does not mesh well with the uncertain work.

There are two primary methods for integrating and rationalizing the different demands of work and the environment. First, *information and control systems* monitor organizational operations and feed data gleaned from this activity to managers and workers so that they can better understand current performance and coordinate activities. Hence, management can coordinate the work with strategic requirements on the one hand and departments can coordinate transformation processes on the other. These systems can be evaluated against the following criteria:

1. The timeliness with which information is provided
2. The accuracy of the information provided
3. The extent to which employees agree to be governed by the information
4. The benefits of the information given the cost of collecting and distributing it
5. The ease of use or the understandability of the information
6. The extent to which the information is aligned with critical strategic goals

An important indication of fit in the organization design elements is the extent to which control and information systems are congruent with and support appraisal and reward system practices in the human resource system.

Second, the *human resource system* is responsible for selecting, developing, and rewarding managers and employees. The firm's strategy and core processes provide important information about the required skills and knowledge that need to be developed through new hires or training and development. Reward systems orient firm personnel to the important issues and represent a primary method for coordinating the information and control systems (that is, performance appraisal) with the human resource system.

The extent to which strategy, core processes, and design factors support each other is the ultimate test of strategy implementation. We return to the Sullivan Hospital System case to demonstrate this process.

---

### Diagnosing the Quality of Strategy Implementation at the Sullivan Hospital System

*The analysis of SHS's strategy suggested that several of its elements did not fit together well, although a strong and widely shared mission represented a solid basis for change. SHS's dominant competence, similar to Westin Short's and other hospitals', was the delivery of patient care. Its particular emphasis, however, was on severe cases and indigent care, and it produced a relatively broad range of services in line with its mission. The hospitals' distinctive competence, almost everyone agreed, was their Level I trauma status. In emergency, life-threatening situations, SHS possessed a series of processes and resources that gave an individual the best chance of surviving.*

*A variety of people at all levels of the organization were interviewed either individually or in small groups to determine the status and characteristics of different organization design factors. In addition, the organization's policy and procedure manuals, annual reports, organization charts, and other archival information were reviewed. This data collection effort revealed the following organization design features:*

- *The hospitals' structures were more bureaucratic than organic. Each hospital had a functional structure with a chief executive officer and from two to five direct reports. Both hospitals had directors of nursing services and professional services. The larger hospital had additional directors in special projects, pastoral care, and other staff functions that worked with both hospitals. Traditional staff functions, such as finance, procurement, human resources, and information services, were centralized at the corporate office. As noted earlier in the strategy section, there were a number of formal policies regarding spending, patient care, and so on.*

- *Its core activity system also could be characterized as traditional. Tasks were narrowly defined (janitor, CCU nurse, admissions clerk, and so on). Further, despite the high levels of required interdependency and complexity involved in the execution of the hospitals' dominant and distinctive competences, most jobs were individually based. That is, job descriptions detailed the skills, knowledge, and activities required of a particular position. Whenever any two departments needed to coordinate their activities, the work was controlled by standard operating procedures, formal paperwork, and tradition.*

- *Information and control systems were old and inflexible. From the staff's perspective, and to some extent even middle management's, little, if any, operational information (that is, about costs, productivity, or levels of patient satisfaction) was shared. Cost information in terms of budgeted versus actual spending were available to middle managers and their annual performance reviews were keyed to meeting budgeted targets. Unfortunately, managers knew the information in the system was grossly inaccurate. They felt helpless in affecting change, since the system was centralized in the corporate office. As a result, they devised elaborate methods for getting the "right" numbers from the system or duplicated the system by keeping their own records.*

- *Human resource systems, also centralized in the corporate office, were relatively generic. Internal job postings were updated weekly (there was a shortage of nurses at the time). There was little in the way of formal training opportunities beyond the required, technical educational requirements to maintain currency and certification. Reward systems con- sisted mainly of a merit based pay system that awarded raises according to annual performance appraisal results. Raises over the previous few years, however, had not kept pace with inflation. There also were various informal recognition systems administered by individual managers.*

---

In general, it can be seen that the uncoordinated elements of the hospital's strategy produced a rather uncoordinated set of design factors. In turn, the hospital's core processes were minimally supported by the organization's design. We examine each of these alignment issues next:

- Did the hospitals' organization support the strategy? This alignment is difficult to assess given the poor coordination among mission, objectives, strategic intent, and policies. If we assume the strategic intent primarily was low cost, the traditional and bureaucratic organization is probably a good fit. The broad product line required considerable differentiation among the departments, including the physical separation of the Level I Trauma Center. As a result, the firm's formal policies and procedures were probably necessary to coordinate the activity. In addition, its centralized human resource systems, information system, and its finance and marketing functions also supported this low-cost intent and served to standardize several policies.

- Did the hospitals' organization support the core competences?

  The mechanistic structure and individual job designs probably worked against the delivery of high-quality care processes that were highly interdependent and uncertain. This is especially true in the case of SHS's distinctive competence of trauma care. In this process, a wide range of medical and technical specialties were required to interact with and mutually adjust to each other and the patient's condition in real time. The individually based job designs, human resource policies, and differentiated departments worked against the accomplishment of the task.

  As in many hospitals, however, the people involved in the trauma unit generally ignored the formal organization when there were patients to be cared for. A group-based, highly interactive team comprising physicians, nurses, and other support staff was formed. Although other departments in the hospitals also tended to form teams as a result of the type of work they performed, the mechanistic organization often caused more problems in these units than in the trauma competence. Perhaps the best example of the misfit between execution of the dominant competence and the organization was the oft-repeated story within the hospital of the trauma patient whose life had just been saved. The patient was left in the hallway for several hours without attention. No one from either the trauma unit or the hospital had processed the information necessary to assign the patient to a room.

- Did the hospitals' organization design factors fit with each other?

  The bureaucratic structure and individual job designs fit together well, as did the centralized staff functions that standardized policies across the system. The one design factor that did not support the other three was the information system. An old system, it was not responsive to the needs of the organization and the data provided by it was inaccurate.

Overall, the evaluation of the organization's strategy implementation showed that the organization design elements generally supported each other and a low-cost strategic intent. The organization as currently designed does not, however, support the efficient and effective delivery of the hospitals' dominant and distinctive competences. The upshot of this misfit is that a number of local solutions had evolved to "get around" the formal organizational policies and to accomplish the work. Such innovations, however, probably added cost to the system, since people resisted standardization and the corresponding implication that low cost meant low-quality care. This misfit also explains the many complaints and confusing signals heard during the strategy assessment.

## Summary

In this chapter, we described the activities associated with diagnosing an organization's current strategic orientation ($S_1/O_1$). In combination with the VIP Process discussed in Chapter 3, the second activity concerns understanding the firm's current strategy orientation. Assessing the quality of the organization's strategy formulation involves first describing the mission, goals and objectives, strategic intent, and functional policies. Then, the alignment of these strategic elements with each other and with the environment is evaluated. An assessment of the quality of strategy implementation requires a description of the firm's core processes and the extent to which the strategy, core processes, and organization design elements align and support each other. This set of diagnostic information provides valuable inputs into the second step of the ISC process, strategy making.

# 5

# The Process of Strategy Making: Visioning and Choice

This is the first of two chapters on strategy making. It represents the second major step in the ISC process. Strategy making is similar to traditional processes of strategy formulation. However, it has three important exceptions. As influenced by the OD Perspective, strategy making is broader in scope, more integrative, and more concerned with the firm's strategic vision.

First, strategy making is broader in scope. In addition to traditional strategy issues, such as goals and objectives, product/market decisions, financial policies, and technology, it addresses their implications on work design and on structure, information/control, and human resource systems. It considers this broader range of issues as part of the process, not as an afterthought. Second, strategy making is a more integrated concept than strategy formulation is. It takes a systemic approach to the content of strategic orientation, including strategy and organization design, as well as addressing the process of specifying an alternative strategic orientation. Finally, strategy making is more concerned with the firm's strategic vision. Visioning, when addressed at all by traditional strategy formulating means, is discussed as part of the leadership responsibilities of senior executives and not as a tool for formulating and implementing strategic change. Strategy making is used instead of strategy formulation to indicate this broader and more integrated focus. The focus of the strategy making step is shown in Figure 5.1.

In this chapter, we describe the first two activities in the strategy making process, visioning and strategic choice. It is divided into three sections and deals with the more process-oriented aspects of strategy making. In the first section, we discuss the full set of activities in strategy making and describe their sequencing. In the second,

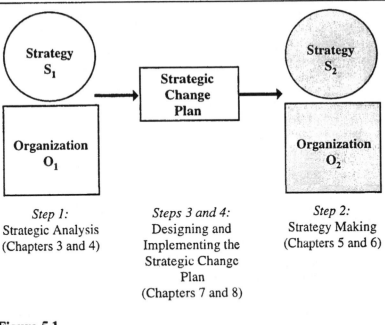

| Step 1: | Steps 3 and 4: | Step 2: |
|---|---|---|
| Strategic Analysis | Designing and | Strategy Making |
| (Chapters 3 and 4) | Implementing the | (Chapters 5 and 6) |
| | Strategic Change | |
| | Plan | |
| | (Chapters 7 and 8) | |

**Figure 5.1**
*The ISC Model: Strategy Making*

we explore the activities associated with developing a strategic vision. In the third, we describe the process of strategic choice, a decision that commits the organization to either revising the current strategy ($S_1$) into a new strategy ($S_2$), adapting the current organization ($O_1$) into a new design ($O_2$), or reorienting the entire organization. In Chapter 6, we discuss the more content-focused issues associated with designing a new strategic orientation ($S_2/O_2$) or specifying the desired future state.

## The Strategy Making Process

The strategy making process takes the inputs from the strategic analysis and formulates a new strategic orientation. The process has three major activities as shown in Figure 5.2 (on the next page):

1. Visioning
2. Strategic choice
3. Strategic orientation design

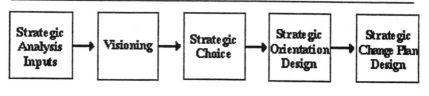

**Figure 5.2**
*Activities in Strategy Making*

The first activity, **visioning**, is the process of developing a commitment to what the organization *should* become and, at some deep level, determining *why* it should make the attempt. The visioning process provides people with an important mental picture of how the organization should look in the future and strong emotional reasons for contributing to the change. This step must address two key, often conflicting forces: creativity and reality (Senge, 1990). Visioning is an inherently "right brain" activity that draws on the emotions and creativity of senior management and the organization they lead. But a vision must honor the present realities of what the organization can and cannot do. Thus the firm's dominant and distinctive competences must be well understood.

The second activity, strategic choice, involves deciding on the type of strategic change to be pursued. It begins by examining the results of the strategic analysis to select the type of strategic change the firm is going to implement. The type of strategic change is described by a matrix that looks at the amount of change in the firm's strategy and organization design. This is an important step because it determines the nature and characteristics as well as the breadth and complexity of the strategic orientation design and SCP development and implementation processes. The strategic analysis, for example, may have revealed that the firm's strategy and organization design are adequately constructed and so only minor alterations are necessary. Hence, it would make little sense to make dramatic changes for their own sake. The firm can adopt change processes commensurate with that diagnosis.

The third and final activity in strategy making is strategic orientation design (covered in Chapter 6). With the firm's vision and the type of strategic change in mind, the firm determines its desired future state. Strategic orientation design can be approached from the outside-in or from the inside-out. Based on the diagnostic model used in Chapter 3, the outside-in approach looks for ways to position the firm in its competitive environment. It rests on the competitive strategy tradition and seeks to ensure that a "good" strategy is formulated in economic terms. The inside-out approach proposes that a firm should build up core capabilities from routines and resources that distinguish the firm from its competitors. Once the strategy is set, then the organization is designed around the core processes. These primarily content decisions are governed by the realities of organizational strengths, weaknesses, resources, and competences. The output of this process is the desired future state of the organization: a clear description of the goals, strategies, resources, work systems, structures, and human resource characteristics necessary to approach the strategic vision.

As with strategic analysis, issues of involvement and participation are actively managed throughout the strategy making step. During the visioning process, a high and broad level of involvement is encouraged. However, issues of strategic choice and many of the issues associated with strategic orientation design are best addressed by senior management.

We view the actual formulation of the desired strategic orientation as a top management responsibility for three reasons. First, many of the decisions fall under senior management's fiduciary responsibility. Second, senior management is more likely than other groups to have the knowledge, skills, and experience to make these decisions. Third, too much participation in these decisions can bog down the decision-making process and lead to missed opportunities, wasted time, and inappropriate compromises that dilute the potency of the decisions.

This restricted involvement in strategic orientation design is not contrary to the OD Perspective. In fact, the OD Perspective plays an important role in strategy making because it suggests that the group dynamics of senior management that were developed as part of the strategic analysis need to be leveraged here. Inappropriate group processes of strategic decision making can negatively affect the quality of strategic choice and strategic orientation design activities. This step represents an excellent opportunity to continue team-building processes that will serve the organization well during SCP development and implementation.

## The Process of Visioning

The first step in the strategy making process is to develop and get commitment to a strategic vision. The visioning process should proceed concomitantly with the strategic choice activity described in the next section. Visioning and strategic choice need to be infused with creativity, boldness, and shrewd thinking. Visions that are outlandish or promote strategic changes that the organization cannot implement are like goals that cannot be reached—they can actually depress achievement motivation. Both of these processes utilize information generated by the strategic analysis, including the organizational realities (for example, existing resources, values and assumptions, and power distributions) that must be acknowledged during this step.

### Developing a Strategic Vision

Developing a strategic vision has become an important part of many strategic change efforts (Robert, 1992). The vision is a centerpiece of most leadership frameworks (Bennis and Nanus, 1985) and a staple in the planned change literature (Cummings and Worley, 1993). However, our use of the term differs slightly from conventional usage. Traditionally, the term *vision* has meant the desired future state, a well-developed image of what the organization will look like five to ten or more years into the future (Beckhard and Pritchard, 1992). We prefer to use the term more in the sense of an ideology, doctrine, or symbolic statement that describes the desired effect, rationale, or outcome of a strategic orientation that has been well implemented. In this sense, a vision is like a goal in that it is something to achieve. However, it is less specific than a goal and, in some ways, impractical. For example, Disney's vision is "creating a place where people can feel like kids again." Obviously, no one can make you feel like a kid, but Disney's theme parks consist of physical surroundings, attractions, and characters arranged in such a way that a person is encouraged to worry less about the "real" world. For our purposes, it is the strategic orientation design step that specifies the desired future state of the organization.

Another key characteristic of an effective vision is that it creates a clear focus on the future through its acknowledgement of the present. If the vision is unconnected with the present, it provides no basis for hope or commitment to change. Apple Computer's vision of "changing the way people do their work" provides a good example of this. Almost everyone has experienced an uninspired boss, the drudgery of a boring job, or alienation in the work place. The notion that one could be a part of an organization that is changing work as we know it into something challenging, creative, or satisfying is naturally alluring. The ability to see the relationship between the present and the future enables people to develop realistic goals and to maintain a perspective of the "big picture."

A vision describes a highly desirable effect or outcome that is compelling and challenging to obtain. It is this sense of what *could be* that delivers both direction and energy. It provides meaning to the tasks people will need to perform during the transition, enables people to reorient their thinking about the organization, and establishes a reason or purpose for their work.

Good strategic visions excite the senses and generate intense loyalty among organizational members. They help to shape choices of business strategy and organizational objectives and guide the design of the SCP (Step 3). They also keep attention focused on real issues, such as competing in the marketplace and working effectively with customers, vendors, employees and others of the firm's constituents. That is, because strategic change is longer and more complex than other types of organizational change, the vision gives people a reason to press on through the difficult transition period.

*Standard Approaches.* There are several techniques for generating strategic visions. Many include activities that get managers to look at their organization in metaphorical terms or from different vantage points. The following questions serve as examples that can kick off a vision development process:

- What should it be like working in or with our organization if everything were going well?
- You have just gotten off the telephone with a colleague. You spent the last forty-five minutes describing why you are so excited about working here. What is it about the organization that made you say all those things?
- It is ten years from now and a banquet has been arranged to honor your organization for its outstanding accomplishments and unique contributions. What is the award you are receiving?

Developing vision statements typically requires accessing the creative side of organization members. As a result, the workshop setting—where participants are away from beepers, telephones, and other normal interruptions—is ideal for this purpose.

From an OD Perspective, there is real value in gaining broad participation in vision development. While it is correct to say that establishing a vision is a leadership function, there is little sense in developing a statement in isolation. The benefits of a good vision as described earlier in this section are not likely to accrue from a secretive, centralized process. Effective visions do not come neatly wrapped, the result of a tidy two-day executive retreat. Developing a good vision may, in fact, require several months. It is 99 percent perspiration and 1 percent inspiration.

Because the visioning process is an important step in the strategy making step, we next present several examples. The first describes the visioning process that took place at the Sullivan Hospital System and emphasizes the role that participation plays.

---

### Developing a Vision at the Sullivan Hospital System

*At SHS, the Steering Committee spent hours pouring over vision statements from other organizations, discussing words and phrases that described what they thought would be an exciting outcome from interacting with the hospital, and trying to satisfy their own needs for something unique and creative. Once armed with the first draft of a statement, they spent several months sharing and discussing it with various stakeholders. To their dismay, the initial version was roundly rejected by almost everyone as being boing, unimaginative, or unreal. The Committee discussed the input gathered during these discussions and set about revising the vision statement. After several additional iterations and a lot of wordsmithing, a new and more powerful vision statement began to emerge. The centerpiece of the vision was the belief that the organization should work in such a way that patients felt like they were the center of attention. Such an orientation to the vision became a powerful rallying point, since many of the hospitals' management team readily understood that there was an existing perception of poor service that needed to be corrected.*

*The six months spent working and adapting the vision statement was well worth it. As it was presented to people in small meetings and workshops, each word and phrase took on special meaning to organizational members and generated commitment to change.*

---

The following example shows how the process can be relatively short and focused within the top management team. Notice, however, that the actual vision development meetings were preceded by some "steeping" time as the managers discussed various statements. There are, in fact, many different methods to developing visions.

### Creating a Vision Statement at Southern Bank and Trust

*At Southern Bank and Trust, the founder believed that the market needs that prompted him to launch the organization still existed. But he also believed that the organization needed more than economic reasons if it were to successfully grow. After several months of tossing around different ideas, he convened his senior management team. They talked about why he started the firm (a story everyone had heard before) and what he believed its core strengths and advantages were. He also talked about the need to capture more succinctly what the firm stood for. The team then watched the delivery of several inspirational speeches, such as Martin Luther King's "I have a dream..." and John Kennedy's announcement that the United States should land a man on the moon. They next discussed the characteristics of a vision statement, after which they split into two groups to build a vision statement. After an hour's discussion, the groups had come up with two short statements that were then debated. The day ended with people feeling slightly frustrated but convinced they were close to the essence of their vision.*

*The next day, group members integrated the statements into one: "Our job is to build an exceptional relationship with every client." It was simple and easy to remember and could be communicated to all organization members. It reflected what the group believed to be the key to success, and was construed to involve both internal and external customers. In working to produce the vision, the founder showed a keen sense of the firm's history and the keys to its success. He also displayed a willingness to tinker with words. All this helped others on the team to figure out what he wanted the firm to become and also gave them the opportunity to determine the final form of the vision statement.*

The visioning process at Withers-Messall involved using the information generated from the VIP Process and shows how these two processes can be linked together.

### The Visioning Process at Withers-Messall

*WM had struggled greatly over determining the basic values and assumptions that drove the business. Eventually, they agreed that the driving force in their organization was a production mentality that suggested "if we can produce it, we should" and that the sales and marketing organization would then find a way to distribute it. For WM, the visioning process started by taking each of the values that had been debated at the earlier workshop and proposing it as the new driving force. Thus it was suggested that the new WM should be customer and user focused, technology driven, profit driven, and so on. Again, almost all of the values had camps that promoted its use. In a breakthrough moment, however, one participant went to the front of the room and drew the following picture on a flip chart:*

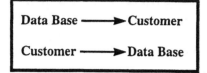

*This person argued that everyone had agreed that WM was production oriented. Such an orientation could be viewed as having a database that was "sliced and diced" in as many ways as possible and "fed" to the customer. She proposed, however, that the firm's mission was oriented to serving the customer's needs and that the customer should drive what's contained in the database. This insight was the impetus needed to transform the organization. It became the symbol of the strategic revolution at WM.*

By the firm's involving others in the creation of the vision, the vision takes on a life of its own. It becomes as compelling for them as it does for its originators. Commitment to the vision is characterized by a sense of ownership not only to the vision, but also to the process to achieve it. It creates a reorientation of thinking, planning, and decision making as it becomes translated into both conceptual models and actions.

***Whole Systems Approaches.*** For firms new to strategic planning, those who want to develop a fresh and new vision, or those who have no vision at all, Marvin Weisbord and others have pioneered a very engaging technique known as a *future search conference* (Weisbord, 1991). The future search conference has as an explicit objective the task of exploring possibilities, not solving problems. To that end, the process involves "getting the whole system" in one room at the same time. Search conferences often include more than one hundred people, including customers, regulators, suppliers, union leadership, employees, and other stakeholders. Through a structured set of activities, the organization begins to appreciate the past, to examine its present, and to vision its future. It is a powerful technique for breaking out of old paradigms and establishing momentum for strategic change. The following example shows how one organization used the future search conference methodology to work on its vision statement.

---

### A Future Search Conference Vision
### for Educational Systems, Inc.

*Educational Systems, Inc. (ESI) is a provider of educational testing services. Changes in the industry's structure—such as increasing numbers of adult learners, admission process reform, and changes in testing procedures— prompted the firm to initiate a strategic change effort. The firm's leadership believed the employees did not clearly understand or own a vision of the organization or how their jobs could positively affect its future. In addition, there was a strong belief that participation by the whole system, not just by senior managers, in crafting a new vision would enable the firm to meet the needs of the educational market. At the same time, such a process would engage employees and allow them to link their personal work to the achievement of the vision.*

*As part of the process, they organized a future search conference to construct a vision of the organization's future. Participants represented customers, suppliers, employees, board members, regulators, and state legislators. Over three days, they discussed ESI's history, its strengths and weaknesses, and its resources for controlling its own destiny. They also discussed the future needs of educational systems and markets.*

*As the conference progressed, the participants began to see how their distinctive competences could ultimately benefit people's acquisition of knowledge and skill. After much hard work on their parts, a vision began to emerge: what ESI really did was to help people become more successful as lifelong learners and promoting greater student achievement was how they should see their business.*

---

## Processes of Strategic Choice

The second activity in strategy making, strategic choice, brings senior management together to examine the output of the strategic analysis. This data is analyzed and interpreted to determine the most appropriate type of strategic change for the organization. In this section, we present a framework of four types of change and describe a process for deciding on the type of change. As stated earlier in this chapter, this step should be undertaken in conjunction with the development of a strategic vision.

### Generic Types of Strategic Change

The ISC model, and the firm's strategic orientation at any point in time, provides the necessary components for describing a typology of strategic change. The typology derives from models of organizational evolution and adaptation. These models (Greiner, 1972; Miller and Friesen, 1980; Tushman and Romanelli, 1985) share the idea that organizations tend to change in one of two ways. They change either many dimensions of their strategic orientation in a relatively short period of time or only a few dimensions over longer periods of time.

Our belief, while simple, is that additional forms of change can be described that differentiate between different types of strategic change. Our primary assumption is that a firm's strategic orientation consists of a strategy ($S_1$) and organization design ($O_1$) that are tightly linked and supportive in high-performing firms. The two systems can, however, be separated in both theory and practice in much the same way that Noel Tichy (1983) unwinds the technical, cultural, and political strands of the organizational rope. That is, some elements of strategy can change without necessarily changing the organization's design and vice versa. While we strongly believe that strategy and organization ought to be tightly aligned, there are aspects of organization design, for example, that are relatively robust and that can support a variety of strategies.

The assumption of loose coupling between strategy and organization allows us to distinguish between three types of strategic change—which are labeled reorientation, strategic adaptation, and strategy revision—and traditional OD or planned change activities—which is labeled convergence (see Figure 5.3). In addition, the matrix in the figure assumes, for purposes of explanation, that strategies and organizational capabilities change in small or large amounts. While there are clearly points in between these two extremes, this distinction suffices to describe the typology.

In Figure 5.3, we have adopted the terms *reorientation* and *convergence* as proposed by Tushman and Romanelli (1985). For our purposes, a strategic reorientation involves a high degree of change in both strategy and organization within a relatively short time. For example, Hewlett-Packard's (HP) reorientation from a manufacturer focused on high-quality, high-priced scientific instruments to a fully integrated computer firm is an example of strategic reorientation. In addition to increasing the range and importance of computers in its strategy, HP made important commitments to the RISC technology and altered significantly its highly autonomous and decentralized di-

Amount of Change in Strategy

|  |  | Low | High |
|---|---|---|---|
| Amount of Change in Organization | **High** | **Strategic Adaptation** | **Reorientation** |
| | **Low** | **Convergence** | **Strategy Revision** |

**Figure 5.3**
*Generic Types of Strategic Change*

visional structure. Convergence, on the other hand, represents low amounts of both strategy and organizational change. In their words, convergence is a "process of incremental and interdependent change activities that work to achieve a greater consistency between strategies, structures and processes and which operate to impede radical or discontinuous change" (1985: 182). Convergence is the predominant form of organizational change and works to better align the strategy with the organization or to better align the elements of the organization's design with each other. Convergence, however, is not strategic change as we have defined it.

In the other cells of the matrix, two additional types of strategic change are proposed that provide interesting variations from the traditional two-category model. A strategy revision occurs when the amount of change in strategy is high and the amount of change in organization design is low. Other terms that have been used to describe a strategy revision include a "change in strategy" (Ginsberg, 1988) and a "strategic adjustment" (Snow and Hambrick, 1980). Ginsberg and Grant (1985) describe McDonald's introduction of a breakfast menu in the late 1970s as an example of strategy revision. McDonald's move was a strategy revision because there were changes in the products offered (breakfast items were added) and the markets served (breakfast eaters) but no change in how work was performed, the organization's structure, or the systems and processes associated with delivering food quickly. True, new people had to be hired and trained, another shift added, and transition plans instituted as the breakfast menu gave way to the standard lunch and dinner menus. But these relatively small issues could easily be handled by the current organization's capabilities, thus characterizing well the distinction between large and small amounts of change in organization.

A strategic adaptation occurs when the organization makes relatively small changes in its strategy but major changes in its organization. Also known as large-scale organizational change, business process re-engineering, and organizational transformation, strategic adaptation involves a major shift in the way a particular strategy is being implemented. For example, in the 1960s and 1970s, most of the major steel firms substituted the Basic Oxygen Furnace, a radical new process technology, for the Open Hearth Furnace. This change required a variety of structural and systems adjustments—including increased structural integration, new human resource and labor management policies, new skills and knowledge competences, and new information systems—to bring about a new implementation of their strategies, which changed very little (Worley, 1990).

Thus the ISC model helps to distinguish between change that is strategic in nature (adaptation, reorientation, and revision) and change that is not (convergence). In line with our definition, strategic change, as distinguished from traditional OD and planned change, is specifically concerned with the relationship between the firm and its external environment. Convergent change is aimed at rationalizing an existing architecture or strategy, works to refreeze or institutionalize a pattern of behavior, or attempts to better align the internal elements of organization design. In this sense, convergence is a process of organizational learning. The important distinction is that these examples of continuous improvement are taking place within a given strategic orientation such that the orientation becomes more and more well defined and integrated. In the other types of (strategic) change, it is the strategic orientation itself that is being altered in whole (reorientation) or in part (adaptation or revision).

## Choosing an Appropriate Type of Strategic Change

The decision concerning the type of strategic change is a most important and difficult one. It is important because a wrong decision—choosing one type of change when another is needed—can lead the organization down a path of poor performance and ineffectiveness. Thus the organization may not change as much as it should or it may change more than it needs to. In either case, poor performance is likely to result. It is a difficult decision because there is no clear set of rules or criteria that tell a manager or CEO which type of strategic change is most appropriate. The resultant uncertainty creates opportunities for political influence and hidden agendas, as well as true leadership and vision, to emerge (Mumford and Pettigrew, 1978).

An important dynamic tension pervades our discussion of strategic choice and should be kept in mind. On the one hand, we will argue for conservatism. That is, too many good strategies and organization designs are abandoned before they have a chance to succeed. We believe there is value in consistency and suggest that a firm revise its strategy or adapt its organization design before it chooses to reorient. Strategic reorientation is a complex, expensive, and risky process that should be undertaken only in special circumstances. On the other hand, there are times when nothing short of a reorientation will do. Making this choice requires boldness and charismatic leadership. This is especially true given the constraints of culture, history, and other sources of resistance to change. It requires a fully functioning senior management team that believes in the need for dramatic change and possesses the resources to pull it off.

No set of rules or criteria has been developed and tested to guide managers into understanding which form of change to pursue. So, we have constructed the flow chart shown in Figure 5.4 (on the next page) as a guide for deciding. We first describe the process and then present a couple of examples to demonstrate its use.

*Strategic Choice and Environmental Stability.* Choosing the appropriate type of strategic change involves several key decisions. First and most important, senior management must examine the strategic analysis data to answer the key question, "Is a major environmental shift occurring or about to occur?" Management must be careful. Reading any popular business book or *Fortune* magazine article could lead one to believe that our world is changing in radical, discontinuous ways every hour. While we don't argue that change is occurring at unprecedented rates, the key question here is whether change has or is about to occur in important and substantive ways, ways that are likely to permanently alter the bases of competition for a relatively long time. This is not the time for knee-jerk reactions to a move or announcement by the competition or to the first sign of a new regulatory initiative. Senior management must make a reasoned and carefully weighed analysis on this point.

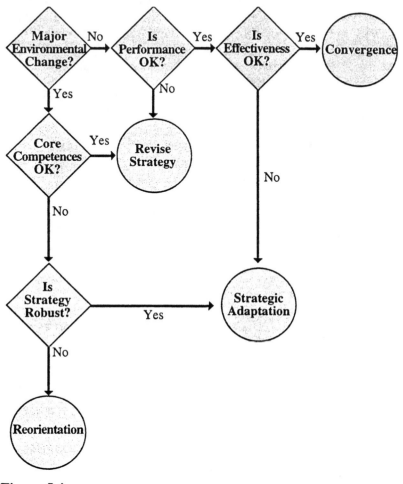

**Figure 5.4**
*Choosing an Appropriate Strategic Change*

Examples of substantive environmental changes that may prompt a "yes" to this question include the following:

- A radically new technology has been commercially introduced to the market.
- A new competitor of substantial size, reputation, or expertise has entered the product/market or industry.
- Economic indicators show sustained increases or decreases.

- A transition in the industry's life cycle (that is, from growth to maturity) is occurring.

In other words, management should be very careful about answering "yes" too quickly to this question. The implications of such an answer need to be fully appreciated. This is, in fact, the primary consideration in moving toward a decision to reorient the firm.

Assume the answer to this question is "no." Then the next question concerns performance of the organization against the established goals. If the strategic analysis step determined that organizational goals were poorly stated or nonexistent, then this decision becomes doubly difficult. In general, however, the question is whether the organization is substantively meeting its financial and quality/customer satisfaction targets. If yes, then the additional question to ask is whether the firm is performing well on other indices of effectiveness such as productivity, employee development and work satisfaction, or ability to handle conflict. If the organization does not anticipate any major environmental changes and is performing reasonably well from both a financial and organizational point of view, then the appropriate type of change is convergence. That is, the organization should, for all intents and purposes, maintain its current strategic orientation and initiate traditional OD/planned change projects to better align the organization's strategy, structure, and process. Organizations that do not reach this conclusion should have at least one very good reason for shaking up its current strategic orientation.

Now, if no environmental changes are anticipated but the organization's performance is not currently meeting expectations, then a strategy revision is called for. The diagnostic model in Chapter 3 suggested that a good strategy is the most important ingredient in financial performance. The organization is most likely to see its investment in change pay off if it focuses on its strategy. However, if current financial performance is adequate but the firm is not producing other outcomes at appropriate levels, then a strategic adaptation is indicated.

*Strategic Choice and Environmental Uncertainty.* If, on the other hand, significant environmental change does appear likely, then two additional questions need to be answered. Compared to the questions on performance and effectiveness, these are more subjective and call on managerial judgment as well as on data from the strategic analysis.

First, senior management should examine the data on the organization's current design. The question here is, "Do the organization's dominant and distinctive competences appear capable of supporting a wide range of strategies under likely future competitive environments?" Answering this question requires a careful analysis of the dominant competence/distinctive competence data.

Two basic issues need to be addressed. First, are the competences capable of generating a sustainable advantage? And second, can the firm exploit likely future opportunities? Responding to the first question requires knowledge about the uniqueness of the capabilities, whether they are valued by customers, and whether they can be imitated by competitors. For a dominant or distinctive competence to be of value to the organization, it must be unique or different from what other organizations can do. Differences are the key to building competitive advantage. The competences also must be valued by the customer or at least potentially valued by some market large enough to support the organization. Here, customer/market research data are invaluable. Finally, the competences must be difficult to imitate (Prahalad and Hamel, 1990). Differences that are valued but easily replicated by competitors, such as price, are not good bases for competitive advantage.

Addressing the second issue, whether the firm can exploit future opportunities, requires utilizing the environmental scanning information. This involves no trick process; it does, however, require some creative and shrewd thinking. One way to think about this question is to determine whether the outputs of current dominant and distinctive competences can be used in new markets or whether they can be applied to produce new products/services. The result can represent important, new strategic ideas.

If the answer to either of these two issues is "yes," then the appropriate organizational response is to revise the current strategy. This suggests that whether or not the organization's current performance is meeting expectations, the organization has certain resources, processes, and routines that can be used to exploit the likely significant change in the firm's industry. Such a condition warrants a proactive change in the firm's strategy, given the current organization.

Second, if the current organization is *not* adequate, that is, the dominant and distinctive competences are not unique, valued, and defensible, then an additional question should be asked. Here, the issue is whether the current strategy is adequate given the current and likely future competitive environments? If it is, then under changing environmental conditions, the organization should opt for a strategic adaptation and alter its organizational structures, systems, and processes. In essence, this amounts to a new implementation of the existing strategy.

Finally, if the firm is facing significant environmental change and its current strategy and organization are inadequate to the task of addressing that change, then a strategic reorientation may be in order.

An example of how one firm applied this model will help to clarify its use.

---

### Strategic Choice at Withers-Messall

*WM's management went through a process similar to the one described in Figure 5.4 in arriving at their decision for strategy revision. To the first question, "Is a major environmental shift occurring or about to occur?", they answered resoundingly, "yes!" The most obvious shift was the increasing presence of the CD-ROM technology as a way to deliver the legal information and to link together the various aspects of that information. This change threatened to result in a major restructuring of the industry, allowing new participants to enter, changing the methods of distribution, and altering the industry's cost structure. Thus the possibility of reorientation was very real for WM. To the second question, "Does the current organization design appear capable of supporting a wide range of strategies under the current and likely future competitive environment?", they also answered "yes." Two years earlier, WM had initiated a drive toward quality improvement and improved customer service. As part of that initiative, a team-based structure had been implemented. That structure was beginning to produce important gains in cost savings and customer service. The division manager and his senior team were convinced it was very flexible and could easily support any new strategies that might be developed, especially regarding the CD-ROM technology. For example, the team-based structure required several departments to coordinate their actions in order to get printed volumes of material out the door. The organization saw this as its dominant competence and believed the team-based structure helped to focus and enhance that competence. To survive, the organization had to turn out high-quality "books" on schedule and on budget. One of their distinctive competences, however, involved their ability to annotate a stream of legal research and cross-reference that information to other volumes or legal disciplines. The team-based design and the opportunities signaled by the CD-ROM technology were seen as natural places to exploit this distinctive competence. As a result, the ap-*

*propriate type of strategic change for WM was to revise its strategy and leverage the existing organization design.*

---

***Linking the Visioning and Strategic Choice Activities.***
Visioning activities and the decision concerning the type of strategic change should be conducted in a highly interdependent fashion. For example, the type of visioning development activity and the scope of change implied by the vision should be a function of the type of strategic change to be implemented. If the firm determines that convergence is an appropriate type of strategic change, then relatively simple visioning processes that reflect the relatively incremental changes to be implemented should be used. If, however, it becomes clear that more radical change is required, then processes like the future search conference that break organizations out of their current paradigms are more appropriate. When the analysis suggests radical change is in order, a vision of incremental change will send an inappropriate signal to people about the urgency of change. Conversely, when convergent change is appropriate, a grand and glorious vision may lead to expectations for change that are unrealistic and that can create cynicism.

### Summary

In this chapter, we discussed the first two activities in the strategy making process: visioning and strategic choice. As with the VIP Process discussed in Chapter 3, these two activities represent important foundational steps to the more content-oriented activity of designing a new strategic orientation, which is presented in Chapter 6. The visioning process is an important activity in both strategic management and planned change. It provides an organization with an emotional and compelling reason to contribute time and effort to the organization. In strategic choice, a difficult decision is required. The senior management team must determine the scope and complexity of strategic change. By utilizing information from the strategic analysis and exercising critical judgment, choices about whether to revise strategy, adapt the organization, or reorient the firm are made. Finally, it is important to see visioning and strategic choice as parallel processes that inform and support one another. While visioning should be highly participatory and engaging, strategic choice is typically performed by senior management. Despite this, the vision should support the type of strategic change pursued and vice versa.

# 6

# Strategy Making: Designing A Strategic Orientation

In the previous chapter, we described the initial activities in strategy making. Specifically, the organization produced a strategic vision and made decisions about the type of strategic change that was needed. This chapter completes the strategy making step by focusing on the more content-oriented issues of specifying the organization's future strategic orientation ($S_2/O_2$). This process is most analogous to classic strategy formulation expanded to include organization design issues.

The chapter comprises two major parts. In the first, we address an important strategic orientation design assumption—that the firm has viable dominant and distinctive competences. Where there are no viable competences, the firm must identify them and then take steps to develop or acquire them before it can begin strategic orientation design. This is, in fact, the most strategic thing an organization can do and is similar to Jack Welch's admonitions, "If you don't have a competitive advantage, then don't compete" and "Know your business engine" (Tichy and Sherman, 1993). This is also important because dominant and distinctive competences represent a vital link between strategy and organization design. If these core processes are not well understood, then strategic orientation design rests on a weak base.

In the second part of the chapter, we describe the process of strategic orientation design—how to specify and align the firm's strategy, structure, and process. The outside-in and inside-out design approaches focus on supporting the competences to achieve competitive advantage and bring the organization closer to its vision. Once the desired strategic orientation ($S_2/O_2$) is described, the organization has a clearly defined future state and can begin to develop and implement the SCP, the final steps in the ISC process.

## Ensuring Strategic Orientation Viability

The process of strategic orientation design involves establishing a strategy and organization that focus energy, attention, and resources on the successful execution of the firm's dominant and distinctive competences. If the process of strategic choice described in Chapter 5 suggests the environment is changing in substantive ways and the organization has a viable set of competences, the firm can skip this step in the process and go directly to designing a new strategic orientation.

If, on the other hand, an organization's dominant and distinctive competences are incapable of creating and sustaining a competitive advantage, then the firm has probably chosen strategy revision or reorientation as the type of strategic change to pursue. To accomplish this, the firm needs to develop or acquire a new set of competences that will yield economic viability. We discuss the three ways by which an organization can do this. With this fundamental knowledge in place, the firm can then proceed with the process of designing the desired strategic orientation.

In developing or acquiring new competences, the organization can choose from the following options:

1. Reengineer current processes and routines
2. Acquire and develop new processes/routines
3. Identify and exploit underutilized resources/processes/routines

### *Reengineering Current Processes and Routines*

Following the first option, a firm reengineers its current processes and routines. This is a popular option in the early 1990s as organizations realize their processes are clearly not capable of delivering high-quality products or services quickly and at low cost. In essence, the organization believes it is in the right business in terms of products/services offered or markets served; it's just that their dominant competence is incapable of competing successfully. This option is designed to quickly bring the dominant competence into the present through the redesigning of the routines. The firm does this by examining the high-level process maps developed in the strategic analysis step and redesigns the dominant competence with "a clean sheet of paper" (Hammer and Champy, 1992).

For example, a developer and manufacturer of branded pharmaceuticals was attempting to understand the threat of generic drugs and determine how it should adapt to that threat. When the patent for a branded drug expires, the drug's price typically drops 40 to 60 percent and is accompanied by a corresponding increase in demand. Thus generics pose a real threat to branded pharmaceutical firms' profit margins. As part of its strategic analysis, the organization developed a high-level process map of its operations and formed a task force to be responsible for crafting an entry strategy into the generics marketplace. Two of the processes—developing new drugs and developing customer orders—became the focus of its efforts. Developing new drugs involved discovering new formulations, testing their efficacy, working through Federal Drug Administration (FDA) approval processes, and developing reliable production processes. Developing customer orders meant the firm had to perform market research, develop product strategies, work with physicians, and acquire customer orders. OD consultants helped the task force map out the key processes and understand the differences between a branded pharmaceutical firm and a generics firm. By studying the generics industry, the task force sought to understand how an effective generics firm would operate. It became clear that many of the processes branded firms took for granted did not exist in generics. For example, a generics firm did not discover new drugs, test those drugs' efficacy, or design production processes. Within the marketing process, it pays much less attention to market research and physician relations processes. Further, the FDA approval process for generic drugs is considerably streamlined.

Additional discussion resulted in a redesigned process that, in essence, combined the two processes into one—labeled drug acquisition and marketing. By integrating these processes, the task force provided a way for the organization, which was used to operating with the costs and risks of long and expensive drug development, to significantly reduce expenses. It also developed a blueprint for the type of organization that would need to be developed to compete in this segment of the industry.

### Acquiring and Developing New Processes/Routines

A firm that selects the second option—acquiring and developing new processes/routines—finds itself without the dominant or distinctive competences necessary to compete in product/markets suggested by the vision. This is the relatively familiar "make or buy" decision. However, developing whole new competences and routines is too time consuming, difficult, and expensive for small organizations that have little slack resources or experience; larger organizations may find this option more feasible. In either case, the organization needs to find new resources. This option is usually accomplished by the firm's acquiring an organization that has the skill and expertise required or by hiring new managers and employees and having them build the competences within the organization.

At LPC, the CD-ROM/technology threat clearly pointed to the need for a set of processes and resources the firm did not have. As it became even clearer that the trend was real and threatened the very survival of the organization, the need for acquiring these resources became increasingly urgent. The organization began scanning its environment for potential acquisition targets. The solution to the problem was easier in this case than in most. It turned out that LPC's parent organization had acquired an electronic publishing firm earlier in the year. That firm, while small, had the knowledge and skills necessary to help LPC enter the CD-ROM market and build up processes for production. Over several months, the parent organization agreed to merge the two firms, thus giving LPC the necessary know-how. After the merger, more people were hired that had specialized technology experience, thereby enabling LPC to develop the appropriate processes for the current market as well as to identify the emerging technologies that might represent future processes. Thus LPC was able to find the necessary resources close to home, while also positioning itself to take advantage of next generation technologies so that it would not have to go through the process again.

### Exploiting Underutilized Resources/Processes/Routines

With this third option, the organization identifies its resources and routines and then finds a creative new way to apply them. This method requires some "out-of-the-box" thinking—the ability to see processes and resources in fundamentally new applications. For example, Nike generates an enormous amount of "waste" in the form of rubber composite materials that make up the soles of its shoes. A group at Nike came up with the idea of using this waste to build running tracks. Hence the firm entered a whole new product/market. Here, the underutilized routine was the disposal of waste materials. The people at Nike found a clever way to make this non-value-added process into a strategic initiative

A Hollywood version of this process is depicted in *Other People's Money,* which starred Danny DeVito as "Larry the Liquidator." In the movie, Larry buys up the stock of New England

Wire and Cable and forces a proxy fight between himself and the incumbent management, vowing to sell off different parts of the firm if he wins. After Larry wins the proxy fight, the firm's employees offer to buy back the shares at a profit to Larry. It turns out that the firm's processes for making wire and cable could also produce a wire mesh required for supplemental restraint systems (airbags) in automobiles.

A final example is provided by the Williams Company, a maker of pipeline for transporting oil and gas. The Williams Company, compared to other, larger suppliers, found itself at a strategic disadvantage in terms of cost and service. Faced with the prospect of acquisition or liquidation, the firm's management looked about for other markets. In a move that looks obvious in retrospect, the firm discovered that its piping was perfect, in terms of composition and sizes, for housing fiber optic cable. Its years of manufacturing expertise, in comparison to that of suppliers in the cable-TV and telecommunications industries, allowed it to enter the fiber optic industry with a cost advantage and helped turn the organization around.

Once the organization has a clear sense that it has or can acquire a set of competences on which to build competitive advantage, it can move to the process of designing and specifying its future strategic orientation.

## General Approaches to Strategic Orientation Design

The next two sections describe a generic strategic orientation design process that alters both strategy and organization, much like a reorientation would. An *outside-in approach* is used when the organization is attempting a strategy revision; an *inside-out approach* works best for strategic adaptations. In either case, the process of strategic orientation design is a coordinated, systemic approach to specifying the desired future state that will best approach the firm's vision.

The outside-in approach proposes that the best way to revise a firm's strategic orientation (in particular its strategy) is to look for ways to position the firm in its competitive environment. It is based in the competitive strategy tradition and seeks to ensure that a "good" strategy is formulated in economic terms. The process involves describing the firm's mission, goals and objectives, strategic intent, and functional policies within the constraints and opportunities posed by its vision, culture, industrial and competitive context, and dominant and distinctive competences.

The inside-out approach proposes that the best way to adapt an organization's strategic orientation (in particular its organization design) is to build up core capabilities from routines and resources that distinguish it from its competitors. Given a particular strategy and set of competences, the organization's structures, human resource systems, and work are designed around those competences. These primarily content decisions are governed by the realities of organizational strengths, weaknesses, resources, and competences.

Both approaches require the firm to be clear about what it can and cannot do well. This is the essence of the resource-based view of strategy (Peteraf, 1993; Barney and Ouchi, 1985; Grant, 1992). This strategy requires the firm to understand its resources, routines, and capabilities, as well as how it might be configured to achieve competitive advantage. Such knowledge provides the organization with valuable information about those strategies and objectives it can implement, and those it cannot. Perhaps more important, this strategy helps the firm to identify those resources it will have to acquire or develop if it is to implement new strategies.

The output of strategic orientation design is a clear description of the goals, strategies, resources, work systems, structures, and human resource characteristics necessary to approach the strategic vision.

## The Outside-In Approach to Strategic Orientation Design

The process of designing a firm's strategic orientation from the outside-in is shown in Figure 6.1. There are four inputs to the process:

1. The firm's strategic vision
2. The firm's cultural values and assumptions
3. Environmental and industry characteristics
4. The firm's dominant and distinctive competences

Together, these describe the firm's hopes, its identity, its industrial context, and its capabilities. Within that context, the organization's mission, goals and objectives, and strategic intent are derived. It is the tension among these four inputs that provide the opportunity for creativity on the one hand and the setting of realistic strategies on the other. A second set of activities becomes more involved with the details of strategy formulation, as follows:

1. Articulating strategic initiatives
2. Establishing functional policies to support the initiatives

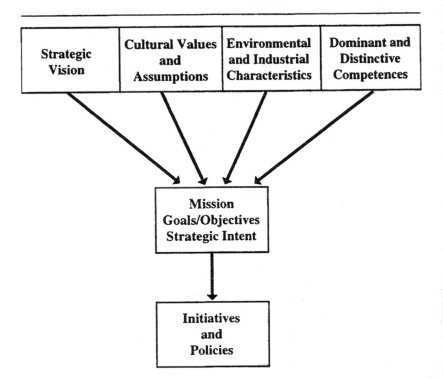

**Figure 6.1**
*The Outside-In Process of Strategic Orientation Design*

We next describe each step and follow each with a short case example to demonstrate its application.

### Designing the Mission, Goals and Objectives, and Strategic Intent

When designing the firm's mission, goals and objectives, and strategic intent, the firm asks, what *constellation* of these elements will best approach its vision within the constraints of culture, context, and competences?

A deep understanding of all these inputs provides the information the firm needs to describe mission, goals, and intent.

*Ratify the Mission.* The firm first should ensure the organization's mission lines up with the opportunities and threats in the environment, supports the vision, and is served well by the firm's dominant and distinctive competences. Obviously, if the organization has no mission statement, then developing one is paramount. The characteristics of a mission statement as described in Chapter 4 should be used to guide the process.

Here, senior management asks whether the present mission is sufficient given the industry's current structure and rate and direction of change. This is an important step because it determines the primary positioning statement of the firm. Will the firm develop, manufacture, market, and distribute a product, or will it simply develop and manufacture? Such statements provide important boundaries for setting goals and strategic intent.

If the strategy is being revised because of changes in the environment, then the scope of the mission may need to be addressed and issues of corporate strategy (for example, what businesses should the firm participate in) included with issues of business strategy.[1] For example, if the industry is transitioning from growth to maturity, such a change may signal the need to diversify. That is, the firm should either offer its services in new markets, develop new services, or both.

---

[1] Corporate strategy involves decisions about the range and types of businesses a firm participates in. These decisions are usually reflected in a mission statement that outlines the scope of industries, markets, and goods/services offered. The decision to extend the scope of the firm's products, markets, and businesses is the subject of consistent and spirited debate. Our interpretation of this literature is that firms that choose to pursue diversification (that is, enter into value chains that are substantively different from their current industry) should do so in a related fashion, with full knowledge of their resources and distinctive competences. Managers should be particularly cautious about diversifying outside of their value-added chain of activities.

For example, JWP built, via related acquisitions, an impressive technical services firm in the late 1980s and early 1990s. However, in 1989, it purchased Businessland Computer Stores, a large retail chain. JWP had little expertise or knowledge in retailing and, despite the great acquisition price, Businessland began siphoning large amounts of cash from the technical services business, where cash and billing cycles were crucial to success. Wall Street recognized this misfit, and as a result, JWP stock fell precipitously. This fall led to JWP's divestiture of Businessland and, eventually, to its bankruptcy. Several studies indicate that firms that start down the diversification path (1) often have difficulty in changing the pattern of decision making (Rumelt, 1974), (2) tend to make more bad acquisitions than good ones (Porter, 1987), (3) tend to divest more businesses than they acquire (Porter, 1987), and (4) tend to have stockholder returns that are not as good as those of more focused firms (Grant, 1992).

The primary focus of the ISC model is on business strategy or competing effectively over time in a particular (or limited range of) product/market, including moderate amounts of vertical integration. Therefore we assume the firm's mission relates specifically to particular products/services and markets. Firms interested in diversification should consult other sources and adapt this process to those issues.

In addition, the firm should compare its mission against the vision of the organization and its core competences. Does it properly position the firm within its industry in order to make achievement of the vision possible? Do the firm's dominant and distinctive competences work well within that competitive position?

In keeping with the conservative bias described in Chapter 5, we generally advocate maintaining the current mission as much as possible. Consistency in strategy, especially in the context of changes in the economy, products, customers, and so on, provides an important steadying influence for an organization. Thus we can envision considerable changes in strategic intent and business policies even if the mission stays relatively stable. In keeping with the OD Perspective, the key system alignment issue is whether the mission is in concert with the organization's vision.

*Develop Goals and Objectives.* Second, the firm should develop, in appropriate areas, the goals and objectives that are aggressive enough to achieve the firm's vision and mission but that also recognize its cultural and competency constraints. In many cases, organizations set goals in two areas: financial and stakeholder. Financial goals concern issues such as earnings growth, various return measures (for example, ROI, ROA, ROS, and ROE), sales growth, and productivity. Stakeholder goals involve various measures of stakeholder satisfaction, such as market share and customer perceptions of product/service quality. An organization should strive to have goals in both areas (Drucker, 1954) in order to avoid a short-term financial orientation that blinds the organization to the need for long-term investment (Hayes and Abernathy, 1980). An important test is to look at the new goals and ask if they are internally consistent. That is, does the accomplishment of financial objectives hinder the accomplishment of stakeholder objectives or vice versa?

*Determine Strategic Intent.* Third, the firm should determine its strategic intent. This final part of this process is very important. The description of goals and objectives establishes the firm's aggressiveness and provides a context for specifying its strategic intent. That is, strategic intent describes how the firm will compete in the market place and the *way* it will achieve its goals and objectives. It represents the organization's "grand" or "umbrella" strategy and should be captured in a short, simple phrase, such as "we are a differentiated firm" or "our orientation is toward low costs" or "we are building the business." The statement of strategic intent should be clear enough to complete the sentence, "We will accomplish our goals of...by... ." For example:

- We will accomplish our goal of doubling sales in three years by building the (computer, consulting, quick-service) business.

- We will accomplish our goal of a 5-percent increase in gross profit margins, by differentiating our services.

- We will accomplish our goal of maintaining our market share at 23 percent by lowering costs in all areas.

In each example, the goal implies and is supported by the strategic intent. For example, the goal of doubling sales fits with the build strategy. All things being equal, an organization will have a tough time doubling sales in a short time frame by differentiating its services. Goals and strategic intents that support one another are an important indicator of alignment.

Organizations that choose strategic intents that are moderately to significantly different than their existing ones should do so most carefully. In many cases, this choice implies the need for a very different set of resources and dominant/distinctive competences. As a result, the firm's management will want to examine carefully the activities necessary to develop or acquire these new resources/competences and the costs associated with doing so. Most management teams underestimate the difficulty, time, and costs of changing their resource profiles to support a new strategic intent. Again, our advice is to "stick to the knitting" by recognizing what the organization does well and leveraging that competence. On the other hand, strategy revisions due to dramatic environmental changes often warrant more of a change in strategic intent than do revisions due to poor performance.

---

### Revising Mission, Goals, and Intent at Withers-Messall

*The key component of the WM vision was the desire for a new customer service orientation to pervade the organization. In the breakthrough moment described in Chapter 5, the organization saw itself as driven by the customer, rather than by the database that had earlier defined it.*

*Its dominant competence was its ability to produce and distribute a large amount of written work, while its distinctive competence was its ability to annotate a large stream of legal thought. In the face of the technological threat represented by the CD-ROM, its management believed its flexible, team-based organization could exploit its distinctive competence and adapt its dominant competence to include outputting their ideas into a new format: the CD-ROM product. With these two pieces in place, they set about the task of specifying their mission, goals and objectives, and strategic intent.*

*To accomplish this, the firm sponsored a two-day workshop. The agenda followed the process suggested above. That is, the senior management team would, in the context of the vision and competences of the organization, first review and ratify the mission. Then new goals and objectives would be established and finally a strategic intent formulated.*

*WM's mission had been developed two years earlier as part of its reorganization efforts. Senior management agreed it accurately displayed the firm's long-term purpose, its reason for being, the scope of its operations, and the external perspective justifying its existence. For example, the mission statement clearly stated that WM existed to serve the legal market and that its success was judged in terms of how well it served that market. Thus, despite management's intention to reshape their strategy in dramatic ways, they saw no need to alter the firm's mission statement.*

*The goals and objectives, however, required a little more work. Although the firm had been publishing a CD-ROM product for several years, that product was clearly not an important part of the business. This was reflected in the prior year's goals. There were clear one-year goals for division sales, operating income, and margins, but no longer-term goals, no goals associated with stakeholder satisfaction (despite its importance being clear in the mission statement), and no goals associated with the CD-ROM product line.*

*Prior to the workshop, the OD consultant and the firm's president talked about what was desirable and what was feasible with respect to goal setting. Having goals that touched several areas (financial, stakeholder, and specific products) and more than one time horizon was desirable but not feasible. For one reason, the parent organization had a strong influence over, and a strong preference for, financially oriented one-year goals. Second, the president felt that since the industry and WM's markets were changing so rapidly, it made little sense to set goals too far into the future. Third, he worried that there were really no control mechanisms in place to measure customer satisfaction. Given these issues, he worried that goal setting might get bogged down in the workshop group.*

*The workshop group discussed this situation and, after some debate, agreed that overall financial goals set by the parent firm would be used to guide product objectives, including financial objectives for the CD-ROM product line. In this way, WM could meet not only the parent's needs, but also their own for operational planning purposes (see the next example for how they did this). In addition, they agreed that one of their goals should be to establish a control system for measuring and monitoring customer satisfaction and to collect this data regularly. This objective actually became a part of the SCP, where objectives for the change effort are established alongside business objectives (see Chapter 7). Thus the parent firm's goals of sales growth and net income growth became the "mark on the wall" that had to be hit by some combination of sales and income from each of the product lines, including the CD-ROM format.*

*Finally, the team saw little reason to shift its current strategic intent of differentiation. They faced a large competitor who had clearly staked out a low-cost position, and WM's distinctive competence was clearly acknowledged as powerful by the industry. Thus the new emphasis on the CD-ROM product and the new vision of customer orientation clearly played into the differentiation strategy.*

---

### Articulating Strategic Initiatives and Policies

A firm's mission, goals, and strategic intent are used to generate strategic initiatives and policies that can guide its development of an SCP.

***Select an Appropriate Set of Initiatives.*** Selecting initiatives is really an extension of the establishment of strategic intent, but at a finer-grained level of analysis. Once the firm establishes the general *way* it will accomplish its objectives, it must then articulate the more specific tactics and methods. First, the firm—given its vision, values and assumptions, and strategic intent—generates several plausible alternatives for achieving its mission and objectives. One such alternative is usually a continuation of the existing strategy with only incremental changes or improvements (assuming the strategic intent has not changed). The other alternatives are usually more aggressive and involve higher levels of risk, investment, and policy changes. Then the alternatives are debated until a consensual strategic initiative is agreed to. For example, Intel faced an important set of strategic decisions in the mid-1980s concerning its "service business" (Lurie, Huston, and Yoffie, 1989). The service business was a relatively unfocused division that sold enhancement products (for example, math coprocessors), developed supercomputer technology, and made personal computers (PC) that were sold to original equipment manufacturers. Several viable alternatives emerged, including keeping things the way they were (status quo), making a strong entry into the branded PC market, initiating a strong entry into the branded workstation market, and harvesting or selling the division. Each option had very strong pros and cons that were debated at all levels of the organization and served to clarify the strategic issues the firm faced.

These alternative strategies can also be evaluated through financial methods. In almost all strategic management processes, there comes a time when the most attractive alternatives are laid side-by-side with forecasts of revenues and expenses attached to each. These options are either ranked and then funded as far down the list as the available funds will stretch, or they are split into two categories: those that meet the firm's "Hurdle Rate of Return" and those that don't. Supposedly, those above the hurdle rate are funded and those below are dropped, within the constraint of available investment capital. From our perspective, two relevant issues work to push this process away from rationality. First, most firms rely more on who is responsible for a project than the actual numbers, since the calculation of present values is vitally dependent on the assumptions that underpin the process. Second, it is more important to initiate changes that are congruent with the vision, strategic intent, values and assumptions, and competences of the firm than initiate a project with a high net present value.

***Establish Functional Policies to Support the Initiatives.*** Last, the firm specifies functional and other business policies that will act as decision-making guidelines for implementation. These may include commitments to a certain level of R&D spending, pricing, advertising, plant and equipment or other capital investments, training, and so on. These may also include commitments to strategic human resource development programs, especially when the new distinctive competences are being employed.

---

### *Initiatives and Policies at Withers-Messall*

*In the final part of the two-day workshop, WM's senior management team worked hard to nail down several important issues. First, as noted in the earlier example, the team used the overall financial objectives to help them set product line-by-product line strategies, as well as revenue and profit targets. For example, the CD-ROM product line clearly warranted a "build" strategy, implying that the firm would forgo profits in the short term in an effort to grow sales and market share. In line with that strategy, sales revenue targets over the next three years were expected to grow faster than operating income. This meant, of course, that other product lines had to pick up the slack in terms of income growth and therefore warranted more "harvest"-like strategies.*

*Once these product line strategies and objectives were developed, the team was able to look across all of the product lines and derive a set of strategic initiatives and policies that were necessary to realize the goals and strategies. First, in line with their vision, the firm needed to become customer-driven. This involved immersing themselves in the customer's world and building internal and external systems to capture customer trends, expectations, and satisfaction levels. Second, building the CD-ROM product line meant directing significant investment dollars toward new product development efforts. Third, aligning the organization's dominant competence to the new vision required recreating and redesigning the existing database. This meant finding ways to develop a cache of information organized in such a way that it could be "sliced and diced" the way the customer wanted, not the way it could be produced. These initiatives were supported by a new set of policies. These included allocating a larger percentage of sales revenue to new product development, adjusting pricing strategies to match product line strategies, and altering sales force compensation to align with product strategies. The new policies also included being attuned to hiring staff with new, high technology skill sets and supporting organizational teams that contributed to costs savings, new product development, or customer satisfaction measurement.*

---

## The Inside-Out Approach to Strategic Orientation Design

The process of designing an orientation from the inside-out is shown in Figure 6.2 and involves the definition of the structural, information/control, core activity, and human resource systems. These systems are designed to allocate and focus resources on the implementation of the strategy (mission, goals and objectives, strategic intent, and policies) and the efficient execution of the dominant and distinctive competences. The design of these systems is driven by the firm's strategic vision and facilitated or constrained by the organization's culture and environmental context. As can be seen, the contextual inputs serve as both criteria and constraint. That is, the desired future organization design must be capable of meeting the organization's strategic objectives and vision but must do so within the capabilities and resources of the firm. Thus the primary purpose of strategic adaptation activities is to develop structures and processes capable of carrying out the firm's strategy.

Unlike the outside-in process, which is driven more by senior management, the inside-out process is better implemented if it includes broad participation in the organization. Because it is the organization design that determines employees' day-to-day environment, their involvement in its specification is highly desirable.

The general process of strategic adaptation begins with a clear notion about the organization's design context (vision, culture, strategy, competences, industry structure). These need to be examined for (1) the functional and technical emphases intended by management and (2) the environmental, cultural, and resource constraints that may be implied. For example, if the strategic intent of the organization is to be a low-cost provider, then marketing and new product development are not likely to be favored functions. If this intent represents a considerable departure from prior orientations, then it is likely to be resisted culturally and the power and political ramifications of such a stance must be accounted for appropriately in the design. Under such conditions, organization designs that require significant investments in financial controls or process R&D may threaten the prior status of other departments more favored in prior orientations.

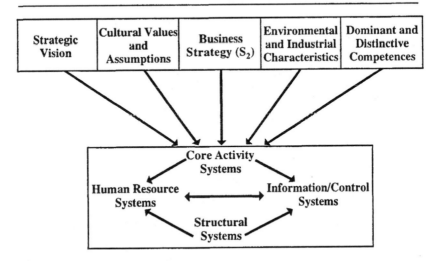

**Figure 6.2**
*The Process of Organization Design*

Once the design context issues have been clarified, then an organization design team can focus on the specification of each system and the fits or alignments between them. More specifically, the organization design should work to create

1. a fit between strategy and the organization design,
2. fits between the four different elements of organization design (that is, structural, human resource, information/control, and core activity systems), and
3. information flows that determine agenda and action priorities that match the organization's situation and the context in which implementation must occur.

Which of the four elements the group works on first is somewhat arbitrary, since they all exist in a dynamic equilibrium. However, the data collected as part of the strategic analysis and the decision process that led to strategic adaptation should provide clues about the system that needs the most attention. Notice that in Figure 6.2, we assume core activity systems—the way work is designed—and structural systems are the primary drivers of human resource and information/control systems.

Thus, in the sections that follow, we first describe the issues and processes that might be considered in designing core activity systems and structural systems. Our bias is to begin with these systems depending on the proximate cause of strategic adaptation. If adaptation is being attempted because of environmental change, then we would start with structural systems. If adaptation is because of problems with quality, work satisfaction, or other measures associated with the execution of dominant and distinctive competences, then beginning with core activity systems makes the most sense. Human resource and information/control systems, seen here as the primary methods for integrating the four systems, are addressed last.

### The Process of Organization Design

The process of specifying these four elements involves the following steps:

1. Describe the current organization design as discovered during strategic analysis.
2. Describe how the current systems' outputs and characteristics compare with desired outputs or characteristics.
3. Specify the required systems' changes.

We demonstrate this process by returning to the Sullivan Hospital System case.

---

### Organization Design at the Sullivan Hospital System

*At SHS, all of the organization's systems needed attention. This is consistent with most TQM implementations. Over a three-month period, the Steering Committee had to make choices about which systems to intervene in first, how aggressively to intervene, and so on. Their first actions addressed the structural and core activity systems. As with most hospitals, its primary structure was functional and consisted of nursing (for example, surgery, ICU, and admissions), professional services (for example, radiology, pharmacy, and labs), and support services (for example, housekeeping, engineering, and food services) departments. The Committee's overriding dilemma was how to focus attention and resources on the quality effort within this functional orientation. In essence, the dominant competence of providing patient care was not housed in any particular function. Each area, in one way or another, touched the patient and contributed to the survival of the organization. As a result, barriers between nursing, professional services, and support services were natural and limited the attention on integration necessary in a TQM-oriented design. With the information/control systems in mind, they also struggled with the problem of how to integrate risk management issues, traditional quality assurance and utilization review issues, and the numerous physician peer review committees that had sprung up over the previous few years. Each of these committees and functions could potentially play a role in the quality effort, but each also reported to different people in the hospital.*

*The Committee's initial answer to these issues was to add to the organizational structure a new department called the Office of Quality. The Office of Quality was to be responsible for implementation of the TQM effort as well as the integration of risk management, quality assurance, utilization review, and the various physician review committees.*

*Second, they addressed the core activity system. Here, many new operating concepts had emerged. Patient-centered care models, shared governance, and self-managed work teams did not match the way departments were organized and operated. In essence, the functional structure at the top was reflected in functionally organized departments that coordinated patient care processes through rules, standard operating procedures, and so on. Under the concept of TQM, such a fragmented service delivery system would not work. So, a consulting firm was hired to work with two pilot nursing units at each hospital to redesign the work. The goal was to understand the current work systems at a finer level of detail (work flow, skill mixes, job descriptions, and so on) and to design and implement a state-of-the-art nursing unit, including full integration with the other organizational functions. After a few months, new design criteria began to emerge that resulted in the redistribution of work across different roles, including RN's, licensed nurse practitioners, technicians, and unit clerks. Although the new design increased the number of full-time equivalent (FTE) employees in the unit, it lowered total costs by giving many professional service functions (for example, drawing blood and ordering medication) to the unit's personnel, thereby allowing those ancillary units to lower the number of FTEs. (Note: This rational explanation should not be mistaken for reality. In truth, negotiating for the transfers of those FTEs was no easy matter, since the professional service managers saw the change as threatening their power base. In addition, the loss of FTEs raised the specter of layoffs and increased employees' uncertainty.)*

*Third, the Steering Committee addressed the information/ control system. Recall that a key performance problem the hospitals faced was their declining market share. While the TQM process would eventually contribute to a reversal of that trend, the Steering Committee and the OD consultants worked out a more direct approach: Address the concerns of the physicians who refer patients to the hospitals. In response to that challenge, the hospitals established what they called the "Physician Quality Council." Once a week, each hospital invited a referring physician to breakfast with the hospital's executive team. After such meetings, the executive team would address issues raised by the doctors and report back to them the status of their suggestions. Not only did this raise management's awareness of key hospital practices that needed to be changed; it also provided the whole organization with customer satisfaction data.*

---

Thus the Steering Committee, with these three decisions, made important strides toward specifying a new design. But they were reluctant to work on other issues, believing such work would commit them to changes that either they did not have the resources to implement or were out of their control. For example, while they did some work in specifying a new recognition system, the really hard work of adjusting compensation systems, performance appraisal systems, and other operating information systems were seen as untouchable because that job was considered to be a corporate function and therefore out of their "jurisdiction."

We have seen this response over and over again. We are convinced that organizations should not stop at this point. In fact, doing so jeopardizes the whole project. Let us demonstrate this point with an example from a strategic adaptation effort conducted at a large telephone company responding to industry deregulation.

## The Advantages of a Thorough Systemic Approach

*Because of telecommunications deregulation, the telephone company's management and union leadership felt strongly that the traditional centralized approach to managing the business needed to change. The outcomes of such a style were a lackadaisical service orientation and little cross-functional teamwork. In addition to coping with the turmoil that resulted from deregulation, the industry was buffeted by tremendous technological changes in information processing and service delivery.*

*An employee involvement (EI) effort was designed to improve employees' quality-of-working-life (QWL) and to increase productivity. A steering committee of senior managers and union officials developed a vision of the EI process and its objectives. To implement the change in this 26,000-person organization, a parallel structure was designed. At the bottom of the parallel structure were employee involvement teams that identified, solved, and implemented solutions to problems in the different work units of the firm. Thus the steering committee specified the desired structure and created opportunities for the teams to address core activity system issues. But they did not address the information/control and human resource systems.*

*Over the next several months, the EI teams tended to focus on QWL issues, such as providing bottled drinking water, upgrading the brand of toilet tissue used, and other "hygiene" issues, rather than on productivity-related changes. Many of the teams, composed of hourly employees and union stewards, rarely interacted with supervisors or managers. Responsible parties within the parallel structure were concerned with this limited focus and so asked an OD consultant to evaluate the process and recommend changes. The resultant recommendations included addressing reward system and accountability issues.*

*The accountability issue was addressed by altering the composition and responsibilities of the different committees within the parallel structure. "Key responsibility units" were formed that represented the different functions involved in delivering quality phone service. At the same time, a new incentive compensation system was initiated that put 20 percent of managers' base pay at risk and rewarded the members of the key responsibility units on the basis of their performance against competitor-established benchmarks and other strategic objectives. Finally, the organization's group of EI facilitators were assigned permanently to functional areas so that they could focus on operating problems.*

*Almost immediately, the EI process began to address cost and quality issues. Managers began seeing EI teams as vehicles for meeting strategic objectives, rather than as distractions. Between 1987 and 1988, an evaluation of the EI process concluded that the program had produced a net savings (after the costs of training, consulting, and dedicated personnel) of over $1 million for a return on investment of over 14 percent. In 1991, the organization surpassed its competition in measures of customer satisfaction for large- and medium-sized businesses. In addition, several organization-level cost measures showed significant decreases. Interviews with various stakeholders indicated that the "revised" EI program was a major source of the improved performance and demonstrates the importance of addressing all of the organization design factors.*

---

Experiences of this type have convinced us that while structural and core activity systems issues are important, the real payoff from organization design work is the improved alignment brought about by addressing the human resource and information/control systems design factors.

In a situation similar to the telephone company's, an evaluation of SHS's TQM effort revealed that the work redesign units, the quality improvement teams that sprang up, and other managers and staff were frustrated by the lack of real, extrinsic rewards and recognition. Similarly, despite the newsletters and other informal means of moving information around in the hospital, most people were ignorant of the accomplishments of the program, could not tell if the program was meeting its objectives, or did not know whether the TQM process had contributed to the hospital's strategy. As a result, the hospital is now addressing these issues.

We think the key point of these examples is that organizations should, at this early stage, think about and specify all aspects of its future design, including the "less important" issues of information/control and human resource systems. Whether such changes occur later rather than sooner is not the issue. The issue is whether the organization understands that all systems must be designed to be in alignment with each other and that alignment is the real key to high performance.

## Summary

These last two chapters have explored the activities and issues associated with designing the organization's future strategic orientation.

Preliminary issues, such as visioning the desired future state and deciding on the type of strategic change to pursue, were covered in Chapter 5. This chapter was more concerned with the content issues of the organization's future strategy ($S_2$) and future organization design ($O_2$). These issues include verifying or altering the firm's mission, goals and objectives, and strategic intent, as well as designing core activity, structure, and human resource systems. In the next chapter, the discussion moves to the design and implementation of the SCP that will guide the organization through its transition to the desired strategic orientation and complete the ISC process.

# 7

# Developing the Strategic Change Plan

In Chapters 3 through 6, we described the activities associated with strategic analysis and strategy making. These activities were analogous to diagnosis in traditional OD efforts and to strategy formulation in conventional strategic planning processes. In the next two chapters, we shift our attention to implementation issues. In Chapter 7, we discuss the third step in the ISC model—developing a strategic change plan (SCP). The SCP codifies the activities necessary to move the organization from its current strategic orientation ($S_1/O_1$) to its desired future strategic orientation ($S_2/O_2$). It includes budgets, schedules, activity plans, and other tools that specify the projects and behaviors that need to occur during the transition. In Chapter 8, we describe the fourth step in the ISC model—implementing the SCP. It outlines the behaviors necessary to actually cause the desired strategic change to occur. It also addresses leadership issues such as making the vision real, providing resources and support, and controlling the process. The relationship between these activities and strategic analysis and strategy making is shown in Figure 7.1.

This chapter is organized around the two parts of the SCP:

1. Specifying the desired future strategic orientation
2. Performing a change requirements analysis

The first part is simply a rational and objective description of the desired strategic orientation ($S_2/O_2$) developed during the strategy making step. The second consists of a change requirements analysis that produces action plans, budgets, and other guidelines for implementation.

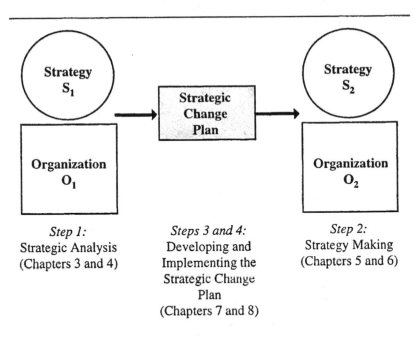

**Figure 7.1**
*The ISC Model and the Strategic Change Process*

According to the ISC model, the SCP is developed after the strategic analysis and strategy making steps. However, an important assumption in developing the SCP is that an appropriate amount of employee involvement during the first two steps makes the development of the SCP a *fait accompli.* Such a process reflects the "go slow to go fast" principle. A strongly felt need for change resulting from the strategic analysis and a strong commitment to the strategic vision developed during strategy making increases the likelihood the SCP will be implemented.

On the other hand, no design process is perfect. While commitment and ownership of the change may be high, the lack of a clearly articulated action plan can quickly dash expectations for change because important issues and change activities were not addressed.[1] Developing an SCP (and its implementation) is explicitly flexible so that as the implementation unfolds, the organization can take advantage of serendipitous opportunities and exploit new information that becomes available.

## Describing the Desired Future Strategic Orientation

The first part of the SCP is a description of the outputs from the strategy making process. It includes the firm's strategic vision, strategy (for example, mission, goals and objectives, and strategic intent), and dominant and distinctive competences. The description also should outline the specific initiatives developed in the strategy making step that will be pursued. These may include, but are not limited to, levels of new product development, marketing initiatives, technological aggressiveness, and financial strategies. It also describes the firm's desired future structures, core activity system, information/control, and human resource systems characteristics. Including the vision statement alongside of this objective description is important so that the reader is provided with some emotional linchpin and the sense of urgency expected during change. Although these specifics have generally been worked out in strategy making, it is important to get these agreements on paper.

An important test of how well the strategy making process was completed is the ease and clarity with which the strategic orientation can be described. If it is difficult to describe or if people disagree over the substance of what gets written down, then there may not be full buy-in to the vision or strategic orientation that will be used. It may be necessary to go back and clarify these elements.

## Completing A Change Requirements Analysis

The second part of the SCP consists of a change requirements analysis that generates several more specific action plans, change strategies, and guidelines. It is the working part of the SCP designed to move the organization toward its vision and desired strategic orientation. These different plans—which include an activity plan, respon-

---

[1] Some readers may wonder if it isn't contradictory to deride traditional strategic planning because it results in plans that gather dust on a shelf and then spend a whole chapter describing the process for writing a plan. In truth, part of the SCP we are describing resembles the traditional strategic plan and may, in fact end up in the

sibility chart, budgets, information plan, and commitment plan—derive from an analysis of change requirements and are shown in Table 7.1. Each of these elements, along with case examples, will be explained in greater depth in this section.

**Table 7.1**

*Elements and Outputs of the Change Requirements Analysis*

| Element | Definition | Outputs |
|---|---|---|
| Specific Changes | The large and small tasks and activities that must occur if the strategic change is to be successful | Activity Plan and Responsibility Chart |
| Timing | How soon, how quickly, and in what order (in relation to other changes) a particular change needs to occur | Activity Plan |
| Costs | The direct, indirect, and opportunity costs associated with a specific change | Change Budget |
| Current Capabilities | The organization's current knowledge and skill with respect to these changes | – – – – – – – |
| Stakeholder Impacts | The stakeholders who are likely to favor or resist a change; the likely impacts on different stakeholders if the change is implemented well | Commitment Plan |
| Change Measurements | The indicators that need to be monitored to determine if the change is occurring | Information Plan |

---

CEO's desk drawer, never again to see the light of day. Other parts, however, are in fact the most important. They are living, breathing, working documents that, over time, will come to resemble a tattered phone book more than a neatly typed, four-color, hard-bound strategic plan.

### Specifying and Sequencing Change Activities

The first, and perhaps most critical, step in the change requirements analysis involves the top two elements in Table 7.1:

1. The development of a comprehensive and systematic list of activities that need to be accomplished in order for the organization to move from $S_1/O_1$ to $S_2/O_2$
2. An appreciation of the timing of the activities

An "activity" can range from a fairly specific behavior (for example, meeting with the marketing staff to discuss coordination of point-of-purchase displays with distribution deadlines) to a relatively large project or initiative (for example, selecting a vendor and implementing a new information system within the next nine months). This is a critical step because its purpose is to prevent surprises. Strategic change is an inherently risky, nonprogrammable, and uncertain undertaking. When one is dealing with the complexity of humans and human organizations, it is a virtual certainty that something will occur that wasn't planned for. Rather than trying to specify in excruciating detail all of the activities that will go on during the change, the firm should be concerned with brainstorming as many of the changes required in as many different areas as possible. Our intent, then, is to minimize the probability of surprise to whatever extent possible. In fact, an important part of implementing the SCP is the monitoring of the process and adjustments to it (see "Real-time Problem Solving" in Chapter 8). The output of this process is a change plan and a responsibility chart.

***Constructing the Activity Plan.*** In a practical sense, we have found that the information generated above can result in an activity plan through

1. gaining agreement on the conceptual categories of change,
2. listing the various initiatives, projects, and activities within each of the categories, and
3. prioritizing and sequencing those initiatives, projects, and activities into a calendar format.

Beginning with agreement on the conceptual categories of activities in the activity plan serves to elevate the initial conversations to a higher, more organizationally focused level. It also eliminates some initial skirmishes over the efficacy of individual activities and allows closer linkages among the vision, strategic orientation, and cultural aspects of the change process. These categories can come from a variety of places, including the model of strategic orientation used in this book. Potential categories include the following:

- New Product Development
- Capital Acquisition
- Training and Education
- Process Improvements
- Recognition and Rewards
- People
- Information/Control Systems

- Market Research
- Technology Assessment
- Communications
- Work Design
- Financial Activities
- Structure

Once priority categories of activities are selected, the identification of specific activities within those categories becomes a routine process of idea generation through some group process such as brainstorming and reviewing/clarifying the lists. Care should be taken at this point to include the strategic initiatives developed as part of the strategy making step.

Finally, the timing of different changes, the ability to change in the short run, and the pace of change are addressed. First, some changes are more important than others and should be implemented earlier. For example, when the firm is reorienting, implementing changes in strategy should probably precede changes in organization design since strategies often set parameters and guidelines for structure and other organization design changes. Other changes, such as reward system changes or decentralization of decision-making authority, are likely to be more effective only after other changes, such as information system changes or new job descriptions, have been implemented.

A second timing issue recognizes that some systems, structures, products/services, and activities cannot be changed in the short run. These include labor contracts, purchasing contracts, fixed capital and equipment commitments, and other relatively irreversible decisions. Third, the pace of change should be addressed. The nature of managerial attention, costs, and information requirements can vary considerably depending on how fast a change needs to be implemented. Some changes need to occur quickly so that they can mesh with other changes. Other activities can be put on a slower track or simply allowed to unfold. As noted earlier in the chapter, there is no way to perfectly specify all activities, since early changes are likely to affect the context and need for subsequent changes. If there is a sense of urgency about the change, such as in turnaround situations, then some changes, which might best be handled sequentially, may need to be implemented concomitantly. This places considerable stress on the information/control systems that will guide the implementation process.

Once each category of activity is developed and sequenced, placing the entire array of activities into a month-by-month grid is helpful as a final test of the overall sequencing of activities. The specification and sequencing of change activities at the Sullivan Hospital System are described next.

---

### Formulating the SCP at Sullivan Hospital System

*SHS focused on five categories for their initial plan: Change Planning, Communications, Training Events, Process Improvements, and Recognition and Rewards. It made a sixth and final category called "Other" available as a catch-all. Several of their initial change activities are shown in Figure 7.2.*

---

***Developing a Responsibility Chart.*** The second output from step one in the change requirements analysis is the responsibility chart, one of the classic and more powerful tools in transition management (Beckhard, 1969). The responsibility chart organizes the specific projects and activities to be implemented by a particular group of people and then arrays them against the people (senior management, managers, other organization members) responsible for making the change happen. For each change, specific roles and responsibilities are assigned. Part of the responsibility chart at SHS is shown in Figure 7.3 (on page 114).

For each change to be implemented, the responsibility chart assigns one of five roles to each individual. (*Note:* The change projects and individuals listed on any particular chart vary depending on the level of change being addressed. For example, the senior management team is likely to be listed for high-level changes, while other responsibility charts for more specific subprojects will list other individuals and change projects of smaller scope.)

The most important role assignment is *Responsibility (R)*. For each change, there is one and only one *R* assigned and this individual is given primary authority and accountability for the accomplishment of the change. Filling out all the *R*'s first is often helpful so that a balanced workload results. At SHS, for example, the CEO was made responsible for the Physician Quality Councils process, while the

**Figure 7.2** *One-Year Change Activities at SHS*

| Category | Months 1–2 | Months 3–4 | Months 5–6 | Months 7–8 | Months 9–10 | Months 11 and 12 |
|---|---|---|---|---|---|---|
| Change Planning | TQM planning session | Develop "Scorecard" for monitoring performance | Progress check | | | SC planning retreat |
| Communications | Plan hospital, board, and physician communications | Communicate to middle managers | | | | |
| Training Events | SPC training for Work Redesign Teams (WRT) | SPC training for Steering Committee (SC) | Culture change training for SC | | SPC training for middle managers | SPC training for middle managers |
| Process Improvements | WRT Pilots begin | WRT / Flowcharting | WRT / Flowcharting | WRT / Flowcharting and customer service audits | WRT / Flowcharting and customer service audits | WRT / Flowcharting and customer service audits |
| Recognition and Awards | | Begin recognition planning | | | Implement recognition plan | |
| Other | Physician Quality Councils (PQCs) begin | PQC Meetings / Patient satisfaction and employee survey results due | PQC meetings | PQC meetings | PQC meetings | PQC meetings / EXPO presentations |

| Projects | CEO | Director of Nursing | Director of Professional Services | Office of Quality | Director of Engineering Services |
|---|---|---|---|---|---|
| Work Redesign Project | A | R | S | I | S |
| Quality Training | I | A | A | R | A |
| Flowcharting | I | I | R | A | I |
| Communications Plans | A | A | A | R | A |
| Physician Quality Councils | R | S | S | A | S |

**Figure 7.3**
*Responsibility Chart*

Director of Nursing was made responsible for the Work Redesign Project. The Office of Quality was assigned responsibility for two activities: Quality Training and Communications Plans.

The second role is the ability to *Approve (A)* (or veto) the contents of a particular change process. While there may be more than one *A* per change, it is best to restrict the number of *A*'s as much as possible. A change that has too many people who can hold up the process makes the responsible person's job that much more difficult. Many managers want to be included as *A*'s for many projects in an effort to make themselves more important or to give themselves more power over the change process. The CEO/President and the rest of the senior management team should work to reduce this possibility as much as possible. At SHS, the responsibility chart suggests that for Quality Training and Communication Plans, the Directors of Nursing, Professional Services, and Engineering Services are to be heavily involved.

The third role recognizes that some changes need to be *Supported (S)* with resources, information, time, people, or money. This role implies that in order for the change to be successful, certain individuals (or their departments) need to be included in the planning and implementation process so that resource planning activities can be carried out to ensure appropriate levels of support. For example, for SHS to meet its work redesign objectives, the Directors of Professional Services and Engineering Services will need to supply resources, initially in terms of people to work on the redesign teams. Eventually, the directors will also need to supply resources in terms of knowledge and skills as well as full-time positions as the new design is implemented.

The fourth role, *Informed (I)*, is less substantive but is still important. In some cases, usually because of interdependencies between functions or work units, a department or individual needs to be informed. An *I* signals that a particular person or unit needs to be made aware when a change is taking place; however, that person or department cannot stop or veto the change. This role is important when many changes are occurring at the same time or when there are high interdependencies between change projects. In this case, *I*'s are important because any alterations to a particular change may have implications for the way another change is designed or implemented. Note that SHS's CEO has a disproportionate number of *I*'s and retains only an approval role for other projects. This reflects his intention to delegate more.

Finally, if the individual or department does not need to be involved in a change effort at all, a dash (–) is entered in the appropriate cell.

### Estimating the Costs of Change

The second step in the change requirements analysis is estimating the direct and indirect costs of each significant change. These costs include the actual direct costs associated with making a change. For example, if the desired strategic orientation includes a new plant or process technology, there are several, relatively large costs associated with buying the equipment and implementing that change. However, it is important to examine other costs as well. These include the opportunity costs associated with a particular resource allocation; that is, any money dedicated to a particular change project could be used in other ways. By analyzing the opportunity costs of a change project, the organization improves the likelihood that scarce resources are being allocated to their best use. Other opportunity costs include the value lost by not pursuing a particular change. For example, if a new work design is being planned, not making that change may result in, say, lower worker satisfaction and lower productivity. Sometimes changes are not important in and of themselves but are quite valuable in that they are necessary for bringing about alignment with other strategy or organization design variables. The cost of misalignment, as demonstrated in the telephone company example in Chapter 6, can be substantial.

---

### The Cost of Change at the Sullivan Hospital System

*SHS simplified this portion of the planning process for two important reasons. First, an overall budget for change-related activities was established prior to the onset of the process, and as long as the parameters of that budget were not exceeded, activities were implemented accordingly. This budget represented the hospitals' best guess about implementation based on various proposals they had received from consulting firms. Second, the compelling need for the change and the shared urgency about the consequences of not implementing it were quite significant, such that the question of "what will happen if we don't do this now?" became a powerful default question that influenced many decisions. Other circumstances also helped to simplify SHS's cost estimation process. For example, the consulting firm hired to perform the work redesign pilot projects (listed under the Process Improvement category in Figure 7.2) quoted a project fee. Similarly, the TQM training was determined on a cost-per-person basis.*

---

The output from this step is a budget plan. Carrying out strategic change requires resources of all kinds. The level of commitment to change and the relative importance of different changes are often signaled by the amount of money allocated to different budgets. The SCP contains three different budgets: operating, capital, and change. The operating budget identifies expenses and investments, assuming the organization is a "going concern." These include salaries, selling expenses, overhead, maintenance, and other common direct and indirect costs. In most organizations, this budget is well documented.

The capital budget contains allocations for special expenditures such as the acquisition of new plant and equipment, computers, process technologies, licensing fees, and so on that are the result of the required strategic orientation. This budget's contents should be carefully thought through for both the qualitative appearance and quantitative feasibility. It is important that the budget accurately reflect the spirit and intent of the firm's desired strategic orientation. It is also important that it be fiscally responsible. Many changes can be funded out of operating cash flows or organizational slack. In other cases, when the changes are more fundamental, acquiring additional debt or issuing stock may be necessary; the associated advantages and disadvantages should be weighed carefully. The change budget details the costs associated with the change itself. The change requirements analysis generates these costs directly.

Each of these budgets, once completed independently, need to be examined collectively for tradeoffs, consistency, and feasibility. The SCP can also be used to help set change budget priorities and timing options.

### Determining Current Change Capability

The third step in the change requirements analysis is to analyze the organization's current capability to carry out the change. This capability can be quite low, especially when the firm is attempting to implement a new strategy that requires new resources, skills, or knowledge. In this case, the firm should double-check its estimates of cost and timing, since these types of changes take longer and are much more expensive. Further, when the organization does not have the required skills and knowledge, it usually means considerable effort will need to be expended on employee selection, training, and human resource development. These costs often have long payback periods, and care should be taken not to discount their importance or underestimate their amounts.    •

The problematic issue here is that, in many cases, an organization cannot fully know what it doesn't know or what it is fully capable of until it is engaged in the activity itself. Consequently, early adoption of a flexible, problem-solving approach toward change is helpful. Following is a description of the change capability issues at SHS. It illustrates that while there is no specific output of this step in the change requirements analysis, performing the step is an important check on the process of developing a realistic SCP.

---

### Change Capability at the Sullivan Hospital System

*SHS senior management had no real idea if they could carry out the changes associated with the TQM plan. While they could hire consultants to lead the educational effort or to help them redesign work, they, as a senior management team, had never flowcharted a process, followed a disciplined problem-solving process, or led a large-scale organizational change. So they made a conscious effort not to schedule too many activities too early in the process and to break several of the steps into smaller units that they felt comfortable with.*

*For example, there was a strong need to begin process improvements throughout the hospital even as work redesign was taking place. They decided against adopting a "shotgun" approach, that is, launching dozens of quality improvement teams in the hope that one of them would hit the bull's-eye. Instead, they decided to first assign managers in the hospital the task of flowcharting one process per month within their departments. This allowed managers (and the senior management team) to learn one quality tool at a time and work with each other on how best to implement process improvements. This slower approach had the added benefit of allowing the organization to pick the "low hanging fruit," a TQM term that refers to changes that are obvious, easy to implement, involve little cost, and promise substantial benefits. By flowcharting many processes, management can identify obvious redundancies or inefficiencies without engaging in more-lengthy and expensive problem-solving processes.*

---

### Assessing Stakeholder Impacts

The fourth step in the change requirements analysis is to assess the effects of change on various stakeholders. Our experience in change planning suggests that doing this helps to circumvent important implementation barriers. This process begins with listing the organization's stakeholders and carefully considering key influencers and implementers. *Influencers* are people who are not involved in the actual implementation of a plan, but who are opinion leaders and therefore have significant impact on the direction and activities of the organization. They are frequently owners, board members, high-status professionals, even key suppliers or customers. *Implementers* are people who actually are critical to the implementation and who are personally involved in this process. Once a stakeholder has been identified, the extent to which that stakeholder is likely to support or resist a particular change can be assessed. Changes that threaten the stakeholder's status, bargaining power, or effectiveness are likely to be opposed, sometimes quite violently. Another way to explore stakeholder impacts is to ask how the change will affect a stakeholder once implemented. For example, the Westin Short Community Hospital was considering a cooperative agreement with the larger hospital at the other end of town, which would have allowed each hospital to obtain some cost savings. Both firms were operating under the specter of health care reform, so such an alliance made good business sense. However, the physicians, most of whom had admitting privileges at both hospitals, vehemently opposed the alliance. They had strong bargaining power and played the two hospitals against each other in order to receive more perks, benefits, and other privileges. Anticipating such stakeholder impacts as a part of planning will yield high benefits at relatively little cost, since failure to do so is a primary source of implementation failure.

The output of the stakeholder assessment is a commitment plan. Commitment planning is intended to characterize the political landscape and to develop action plans to bring about appropriate levels of commitment to a particular change project. A commitment plan utilizes the information from the stakeholder assessment to identify the *key* individuals, groups, and stakeholders either who must effectively support a particular change project in order to ensure its success or whose resistance could cause the change project to fail. Commitment planning is carried out on a change-by-change basis, generally by the individual who is *Responsible* for that change. A commitment plan for the overall change effort may also be constructed. This type of commitment plan is illustrated here, but the process for developing it is the same for other changes. A partial example of the SHS commitment plan is shown in Figure 7.4.

In the figure, each key stakeholder is listed on the left and then the current level of commitment to change that each holds is rated on a scale of 1 to 4. A 1 represents active resistance or opposition, a 2 passive resistance, a 3 passive support, and a 4 active support. For each stakeholder, an X is placed in the column that best represents that stakeholder's level of support. For example, Donald, the CEO of the larger hospital, is seen as an active supporter, whereas the

| Stakeholder | Active Resistance | Passive Resistance | Passive Support | Active Support |
|---|---|---|---|---|
| Donald Fulton, CEO | | | | X⟶O |
| Medical Staff | X⟶O | | | |
| Nursing Staff | | | X⟶O | |
| Corporate Office | X⟶O | | | |

**Figure 7.4**
*Partial Commitment Plan at the Sullivan Hospital System*

medical staff is seen as passive resisters. If the level of support is unknown, there are several ways to find out. The most direct and preferred method is to ask for the stakeholder's opinion about the change.

Once the current level of support is known, the *minimum* desired level of support for each stakeholder is recorded on the chart by an O. It is important to determine the minimum level of support necessary. While having everyone provide active support is desirable, this is an unrealistic and naive objective. Clearly, constructing this part of the commitment plan requires some strategic thinking and an understanding of the "critical mass" necessary to bring change about in the organization.

The commitment plan in Figure 7.4 indicates Donald is an active supporter and needs to remain that way. The two most difficult resisters to handle are the medical staff and the corporate office. Both are seen as passive resisters. They must, at a minimum, become passive supporters. The nursing staff passively supports the process but needs to be an active supporter. Based on these characterizations, specific steps to move the stakeholders to appropriate positions can be developed. Successfully implementing the change at SHS, for example, requires that most attention and resources be applied to improving the medical staff's and corporate office's positions.

A final aspect of commitment planning is to present the completed SCP to different levels and functions in the organization for comment. Although many changes are probably already taking place, providing a formal SCP gives people an additional way to contribute, to participate, and to own the changes that are occurring or will occur. A formal plan also gives people information about the change and sends a clear signal that the change has received careful and considerable thought. Hence, there is less likelihood of cynicism and a greater likelihood that people will perceive that the "left hand knows what the right one is doing."

### Collecting Change Measurements

In the final step of the change requirements analysis, measurements or indicators are generated that can be used to gauge whether the change is occurring. Also known as "implementation feedback," this information reflects the change effort's progress rather than organizational outcomes, such as performance improvements. Examples include the reaching of  milestones on developing new products, identification of acquisition candidates, or the number of groups trained in self-managing principles. Ostensibly, these measurements would indicate that improvements in organizational outcomes are not far off. They can therefore be used to monitor the success of the change process itself as well as provide valuable inputs to modifications of the SCP during the implementation process (see "Controlling the Process" in Chapter 8).

As noted earlier, this control and evaluation system needs to be sensitive to the type of strategic change being implemented. When many changes are being implemented at the same time, the number of evaluation measures increases exponentially, thereby making for a relatively complex and rich information-sharing environment. Change leaders should look for information sources that can indicate progress on more than one change project in order to reduce the information requirements.

In any event, control systems need to be specified so that the implementation process can be monitored. These controls should work in tandem with and support the organization's ongoing control systems that monitor firm performance and operations. For example, if the organization is moving from an individual-based to team-based activity system, then changing the organization's performance appraisal system is likely to be on the list of needed changes. In addition, indicators that monitor the number of work groups that are governed by the old versus new performance appraisal system provide implementation feedback that support the new control.

The output from the change measurement step is an information plan that concerns information collection and information dissemination. The information plan therefore helps to provide the organization with the necessary data to initiate, track, monitor, and guide the change process. The development of this information plan should be one of the changes on the senior management team's responsibility chart. A well-developed plan for collecting and feeding back information about the change's progress is a hallmark of effective change management.

Producing the first part of the information plan involves collecting information necessary for understanding how the change process is proceeding. The change requirements analysis should be examined for the measurements and indicators of change that are listed most often. Commonly, a few central ones tend to emerge and should be developed and monitored for change progress.

Several criteria for an effective control system have been developed and should be used in designing controls for the transition period. These criteria include the following:

- The timeliness with which information is provided to members
- The accuracy of the information
- The ease with which the information is understood
- The degree to which the information illuminates areas critical to the success of the organization/change plan
- The extent to which the cost of acquiring and distributing the information does not exceed the benefits of its use
- The extent to which people accept being governed by the information

For example, many organizations spend millions of dollars on information systems that produce reams of data that is unintelligible to organization members. In many cases, this data is also inaccurate, and yet managers and others are held accountable to them. If the responsible individual can construct an evaluation plan according to these criteria, then the team can be assured the information being channeled back to employees and managers (perhaps as part of the information plan) is useful.

Producing the second part of the information plan involves developing a means of providing organizational members with information about upcoming change events, progress on the SCP, and other information that might help people understand the change effort. This part of the information plan represents one of the most frustrating aspects of change. An organization typically has several channels through which information about the organization and its operations flow, whether these channels are consciously developed or informally emergent. Informal systems of social networks, organizational and departmental newsletters, formal information systems, memoranda, public announcements, bulletin boards, and the like are common. Hence, amidst all the day-to-day noise, communications about important organizational change events and activities often get lost.

Organizations have two choices with respect to communications. If the number of channels already in existence is small, then adding a new channel can effectively communicate change activities. If the number of existing channels is large, then we have found that effective communication often requires reducing the number of channels and carefully "leaking" information through selected channels.

In either case, research suggests the communications plan should consciously attempt to repeat a message frequently and through as many different channels as possible. The implication of these alternatives is that the group responsible for strategic change must be absolutely clear about the messages to be sent and that the messages should be kept small in number and very simple in content.

## Summary

Developing the SCP involves writing down the desired future strategic orientation and performing a change requirements analysis. This analysis provides basic information about the number, type, sequence, and priority of changes; their costs, stakeholder impacts, and measurements; and the ability of the organization to carry out the changes. Based on this data, several action plans are formed, including a commitment plan, responsibility chart, information plan, and budgets. In the next chapter, the elements of the SCP are executed and implemented.

# 8

# Implementing the Strategic Change Plan

In this chapter, we describe the fourth, and final, step in the ISC process: implementing the SCP. While in prior chapters we diagnosed and specified various aspects of strategic change, in this chapter we specifically address the activities that make the vision real, provide resources and support, and control the process.

The best diagnosis and action planning in the world cannot substitute for the taking of action. For change to occur, senior management and those charged with specific change projects must either alter the practices, behaviors, and activities of the organization or cause those to change. Much like swimming upstream, changing an organization's strategy and structure requires persistence and a variety of methods and skills.

In the classical approach to strategy implementation, the emphasis is on the movement from $S_1$ to $S_2$. Changes in product and market strategies are carried out, resources are allocated, and functional plans are designed and focused on corporate or line-of-business objectives. This is not to imply that no effort is given to designing the organizational structure, rewarding appropriate behavior, and monitoring results. Progressive firms employ all of these implementation procedures.

The difference between the conventional approach and the ISC approach lies in the sequence and emphasis given to involvement and participation in strategic analysis and strategy making. In the ISC process, meaningful inputs are received from influencers and implementers so that the SCP reflects *their* values, priorities, and realities as well as management's.

Implementing and facilitating change is the true outcome of effective leadership. So we devote this chapter to describing the activities that the leadership of the organization must engage in to ensure the implementation of the SCP and the achievement of the new strategic orientation ($S_2/O_2$). Strategic leadership behaviors in implementation fall naturally into three areas:

1. Making the vision real
2. Providing resources and support
3. Controlling the change process

Armed with the information and plans in the SCP, the CEO, other organization leaders, and implementers/influencers must commit to action and empower those who have change responsibilities. Each of these leadership behaviors, discussed in the following sections, is intended to cause action to occur, either by "pushing" or "pulling" individual behavior.

## Making the Vision Real

Some of the most important activities the organization's leadership can do is to

- embody, or live, the strategic vision,
- create a context for change,  '
- set high and positive expectations, and
- galvanize commitment.

These actions provide organization members with a clear signal regarding why change is occurring and what is expected of them. They also signal that management is serious about its commitment to the vision.

### Living the Strategic Vision

During strategy making, a strategic vision was created, led by the organization's senior management. The vision is a description of the desirable effect or outcome that would result from a well-implemented strategic orientation or an emotional reason for coming to work. Its development was highly participatory, such that strong commitment and ownership of it should have resulted. Once the organization has committed to change, the organization's leadership, especially the CEO, needs to strongly and visibly support the vision. This is done by routinely and consistently repeating the vision, using the vision in daily decision making, and acting today as if the vision were a reality.

---

### Living the Vision at the Sullivan Hospital System

*During the change process at SHS, CEO Donald Fulton was seen routinely walking the hallways asking people the same question over and over again: "Are we a higher-quality organization today than we were thirty days ago?" He also encouraged others to ask themselves this question everyday. The consistency with which he repeated this message helped people to understand the vision—which saw patient care and comfort as the highest purpose—and to link that vision to issues of quality. At the other hospital, CEO Mary Fenton began "quality strolls." After meetings of the senior management team or departmental managers, and often at random, she and her direct reports would walk through the hospital to find examples of "unquality." Using the "coffee stain" principle made famous by Jan Carlzon of SAS Airlines, Mary believed that if the hospital presented a neat and clean image, then it would be easier for patients and their families to believe they were the "center of attention" at the hospital.*

---

The routine and consistent repetition of the vision has several important consequences. First, it supports the information plan and often communicates to others what the organization is trying to become. Second, it serves as a shorthand description of the desired future strategic orientation, thereby keeping it clearly in the minds of organization members. As different changes are occurring, organization members have an obvious "tie breaker," or singular criterion against which to judge the "rightness" or appropriateness of some activity or decision. They can do the same activity the old way and support the status quo or try it the new way and be a part of the change that brings the new vision into fruition. Third, it represents one element of commitment and increases the degree of trust in management (Bennis and Nanus, 1985).

Using the vision (and the associated mission statement of the strategy) in daily decision making reinforces that it is an important aspect of organizational functioning. Most organization members are used to decision making under an old set of rules, so this practice helps them to understand the nuances of the vision and how it should be applied in making day-to-day decisions.

Finally, it is important, especially for the CEO and the senior management team, to act today as if the vision were a reality. Repeating the vision and using it in daily decision making are two very tangible manifestations of that commitment. However, there are myriad "moments of truth" when senior management is interacting with both internal and external stakeholders. At these times, people are acutely aware of behaviors and language that support, or do not support, the spirit and intent of the vision. Nothing gives organization cynics more ammunition than a senior management team that is not "walking the talk" (Block, 1993).

### Creating a Context for Change

Closely associated with living the vision is the need for leadership to continue to create a context for change that began (one can hope) with the VIP Process, the strategic analysis, and strategy making. Managers need to construct a simple and clear message about how the vision and the desired strategic orientation address the key business issues the firm faces and how they will lead to superior performance. In this way, the organization's "strategic logic" to gain competitive advantage is conveyed. Organization members then will understand why the new vision and new strategic orientation are right and how both will lead to positive performance and effectiveness.

---

### Change Contexts at Withers-Messall and the Sullivan Hospital System

*At both WM and SHS, creating a change context was easy. WM faced a clear threat in the form of the CD-ROM technology. Its president was very good at painting mental pictures of the impact of the technology on the industry's competitive features; many of these pictures did not include WM as an important force. These images reinforced the importance of taking action now in order to prevent undesirable results from occurring later and helped organization members see the importance and urgency for change. At SHS, the increased importance of managed care contracts, the shifts in regulatory requirements by accrediting agencies, and changing industry dynamics associated with health care reform were ample impetus for commitment to the change.*

---

### Setting High and Positive Expectations

Setting high and positive expectations is an important aspect of implementing change. The expectations start with senior managers' living the vision and should flow to all organization members. Specifically, senior managers should model and reinforce the behaviors they expect in others and should set high standards for themselves and for the people who report to them. For example, leaders should not expect people to go through experiences they have not gone through themselves. They can help build rapport by, say, telling personal stories of change. For example, at one organization that was implementing a strategic adaptation, the senior management team developed a decision-making process based on who argued the longest and most emotionally. As part of learning to make decisions based on a new set of criteria—namely, facts and consensus—team members told stories to others about how hard it was to catch themselves at old behaviors. These stories suggested that change would be difficult for everybody and that mistakes would be made as they tried out new behaviors.

Middle managers should be expected to achieve both business results and the changes specified in the SCP plan. Visions often imply that a great deal in the organization needs to change. Translating that vision into expectations requires a deep conviction that the organization will reach its potential only if its people are unleashed. When leaders express their beliefs that unprecedented results will be achieved, they set high and positive expectations of their people. This is accomplished primarily through the principle of self-management. Leaders provide direction for people, involve them in setting performance goals and standards, and then allow them to exercise their own initiative in accomplishing those goals. While the leaders stay involved in planning, management, and the evaluation of results, they are careful not to diminish a person's accountability, stewardship, authority, or ownership. Organization leadership, while realizing that progress takes time, should expect to see sustained effort and progress toward change goals.

### Galvanizing Commitment

Living the vision, creating a context for change, and setting high and positive expectations help to "pull" organization members toward the actions and behaviors that are necessary to make the vision real. The final aspect of making the vision real—galvanizing commitment—is more of a "push" strategy.

Galvanizing commitment involves the senior management team's taking action on the commitment plan, the information plan, and the responsibility chart. By focusing on the commitment plan early, the team engages in "positive politics." That is, it addresses the individuals, groups, or stakeholders who need to be influenced to move from their current position to their desired level of support. As a result, political leadership is coalesced around strategic activities and positive, direct, and visible action is taken.

The team also can "push" to make the vision real by visibly commissioning certain changes in the responsibility chart to begin. This is facilitated by the provision of resources and support.

## Providing Resources and Support

A second component of SCP implementation is the provision of resources and support. This involves

- making the necessary resources—for example, time, people, and money—available,
- championing change, and
- staying the course.

These actions ensure the changes being made are supported properly and that commitment is not withdrawn from the process.

### Allocating Resources

One of the best ways to kill a strategic change effort is to underfund or undersupport critical change projects. Leaders must see these expenditures as investments, not costs. By their allocating resources to change items on the responsibility chart, they create energy and momentum. In this case, actions speak louder than words by sending clear signals of management's intention and support.

---

### *Allocating Resources at the Sullivan Hospital System*

*At SHS, the most tangible symbol of unwavering support came early in the change implementation process: executives refusing to excuse their direct reports from planned training sessions or cross-functional improvement team meetings when those reports claimed to be too busy. Previous change attempts at the hospitals had spawned a prevailing wisdom that handling a heavy current workload was always more valued than participating in training or meetings that might someday result in reducing that workload. Consequently, asking for permission not to participate became the norm. This time, however, such "opting out" was disallowed early in the process. A clear message was sent that the human resource development and training aspects of the change were important components of the vision and desired strategic orientation.*

---

Depending on the type of strategic change being implemented, the role of training and the commitments to training need to be made clear. Training can be a powerful signal of commitment to, and a valuable facilitator of, change. It also can be a big waste of money. A consultant friend of ours characterized the problem as "just-in-time" versus "waste-of-time" training. The right concepts taught at the right time can provide impetus to a change effort. However, if the right concepts are taught at the wrong time, trainees have no immediate use for the knowledge and skills and the impact of the training quickly fades.

Along with the allocation of resources should come the assignment of responsibility and authority. The person responsible for a particular change should be given not only the appropriate resources to succeed, but also the leeway to design the change and implement it under the guidelines established in the responsibility chart (that is, the change must be approved and supported by other specific individuals). Without adequate autonomy, the change project leader will be unlikely to have ownership of and strong commitment to the change project.

### Championing Change

Championing change involves creating a common sense of purpose among the implementers and influencers of a particular change and coordinating the change with other projects. The CEO obviously plays an important role in championing change. Also important are the people responsible for particular change projects. Championing begins with clarifying the desired end state, including standards of achievement, management practices, and time commitments. Champions thus serve as symbols of change by practicing the processes that ensure the success of the change process.

Championing change also requires the achievement and maintenance of consensus among the key stakeholders of each change project. Consensus means critical issues are considered and debated so that the people involved thoroughly understand the significance of those issues and the ramifications of their decisions. True consensus is reached when the stakeholders, after considerable disagreement, reach a strong understanding of the issues and a clear commitment to a course of action. As Argyris (1970) said, consensus requires valid data and free informed choice, essential ingredients for deep levels of commitment.

Leaders also are responsible for aligning their change projects with other changes and with the strategic and business goals of the organization. This is most easily accomplished by their attending to the implications of a responsibility chart. When projects requiring coordination of effort are not coordinated, a change effort can be easily derailed. It is the leader's job to ensure everything proceeds in an orchestrated manner.

### Staying the Course

Finally, strategic management requires persistent leadership. This is particularly true for changes that require perseverance and cover a long time frame. Without someone expressly responsible for watching over the strategic effort and keeping it going, it is likely to take a back seat to short-term demands. The strategic leader must continuously shepherd the process and ensure other leaders do likewise.

This is not as easy as it sounds. Figure 8.1 (on page 132) shows why. Our experience with strategic change in organizations suggests that too many managers believe change "just happens." Consider the scenario in which a chosen intervention, such as strategic adaptation or strategy revision, at time 1 results in immediate and continuous improvement to the desired level of effectiveness at time 3. This is represented by the straight line, *a*, at the top of the figure. The clear assumption underlying this expectation is that all employees and managers will immediately drop their old routines and begin working in ways that embrace the new methods that have been clearly articulated by an omniscient senior management team. Unfortunately, transition models and plenty of experience suggest that lines *b* or *c* in the figure represent the more likely scenarios. The difference between the two lines is the measurement of management's effectiveness in implementing strategic change.

In line *b*, a well-managed transition stage recognizes and plans for temporary declines in performance. We believe an explicit description of this reality, as well as a clear understanding and agreement from the senior management team, needs to occur at the initial formulation stages of any significant change process. It is our experience that this key fact can help an executive team "stay the course" through the difficult and arduous process of change, provided they learn early on that it is predictable and healthy to suffer a decline in performance as new behaviors, strategies, and processes are engaged and old, outdated ones are abandoned. We use the analogy of a burning house to illustrate the process. At time 1, the organization is a burning house, so the firm must move into a temporary dwelling while a new and better house is built. People will find both the interim dwelling and the permanent replacement uncomfortable at first

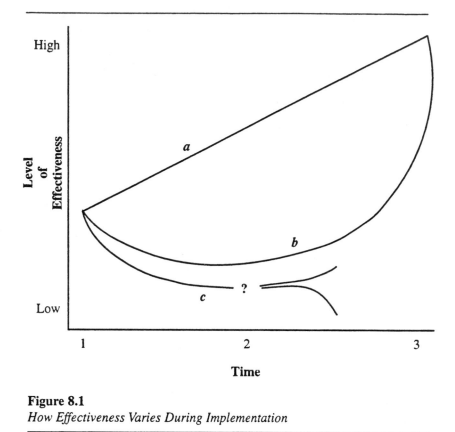

**Figure 8.1**
*How Effectiveness Varies During Implementation*

and will have trouble finding and using familiar things. Thus performance will decline. However, once they move into the new building and become comfortable, their satisfaction and performance will improve. Thus it would be a mistake for them to use their initial discomfort to justify adhering to the status quo when they know the change is important.

At the bottom of the curve, senior management confirms its endorsement of the change plan and redoubles its efforts to support change. Momentum in the organization builds and performance not only rebounds, but exceeds previous levels.

Line *c* represents strategic change that has not been well planned. Performance declines rapidly at first as the changes are announced and the various stakeholder groups resist the new initiatives.

At some time, a point is reached at which a choice must be made. This is represented by the "?" in the figure. Here, management either decides to continue to pursue the new course of action despite the decline in performance or, more typically, abandons the change program. The problems associated with the failed change are blamed either on some uncontrollable external force or on an internal scapegoat that is promptly dismissed. In either case, it is questionable whether performance will rebound or continue its decline. For example, at one organization we worked with, an intense and highly participative strategic analysis was followed by a very short and secretive strategy making and SCP development process. The initial training indicated that a large amount of change would be required to fully implement the new strategic orientation. The change was subsequently resisted by middle managers, who convinced their respective senior managers that no one had the time to initiate the changes. Because of the volume and intensity of the feedback, senior management decided to abandon the change effort. The performance issues that prompted the effort were not revisited for another three years.

All organizational change involves some short-term additional costs, so short-term performance is more likely to decrease than increase. As a result, severe pressure is placed on senior management and the CEO. Their collective commitment to the change may be challenged by stockholders, board members, and other stakeholders. This period represents an important test that we term the "crucible of leadership." During this time, it is vitally important that organization leadership trusts the process that got them to this point. The organization and its members have probably charted a viable and appropriate course of action that will lead to an effective strategic orientation. So there is good reason to believe in the strategy and to stick with it. Also, now it is especially important to utilize the information plan and the activities outlined in the next section to understand the effectiveness of changes implemented thus far and to institute any modifications to the plan suggested by the data.

## Controlling the Change Process

In addition to committing resources and staying the course, leaders of the strategic change need to accumulate and utilize information to control the change process. Control systems collect information about operations, in this case, the operation of the SCP. The information is then compared against some standard, and decisions are made about whether to modify a process. Controlling a change process involves more than just collecting and utilizing information. In this section, we discuss

- engaging in real-time problem solving,
- celebrating success, and
- making change stick.

### Engaging in Real-time Problem Solving

The information plan details the data that best indicates the extent to which changes in the responsibility chart are actually being implemented. In addition, the strategic goals and objectives and the information collected by the organization's ongoing control systems provide data on performance, efficiency, and effectiveness. The purpose of real-time problem solving is to use this data to monitor implementation progress and modify the SCP, especially the activities listed on the responsibility chart.

As information on each change is collected and reported, progress reviews are held at which are noted the accomplishments and difficulties associated with implementing the changes. In addition, decisions are made about modifying a change process, speeding up or slowing down the pace of a particular change project, allocating more or fewer resources to one or more projects, and determining other needed actions. These reviews also cover what learning is occurring, whether actions are consistent with the vision and values of the organization, and how change can be better managed in the future.

---

### Real-time Problem Solving at the Sullivan Hospital System

*Real-time problem solving at SHS took the form of regular meetings of the Steering Committee. These meetings featured reports about various aspects of the change effort and discussions regarding their implications for other changes. For example, as the design of the pilot nursing units began to take shape, rumors emerged suggesting that work redesign was going to produce layoffs. In response, several nurses raised the issue of whether a union organizing effort might be their best course of action. The Steering Committee subsequently modified their information plan, addressing the layoffs concern as well as providing more information about the work redesign efforts. The Committee also spent time discussing how the situation had developed and how similar situations could be avoided in the future.*

---

### Celebrating Success

An important element in controlling the process is recognizing and rewarding accomplishments. This reward and recognition process should not be taken lightly. Trivial attempts at recognition, such as T-shirts, lapel pins, and the like, are quickly dismissed by organization cynics and bystanders. This is not to say, however, that such rewards do not have their places. One organization hit on the idea of awarding massages to managers who completed their assigned change projects. This prize was not only different and highly valued, it also addressed the stress levels created by the change effort.

In navigating an organization through strategic change, the celebration of accomplishments needs to be seen as an important event. Visible, substantive awards for achievement send important signals about the types of behaviors and accomplishments expected in accordance with the vision and the new strategic orientation. The individuals or departments that are singled out should represent role models for the rest of the organization. For example, if the new strategic orientation represents a shift from individual-based to team-based work, it is important to reward a group.

---

### Celebrating Success at the Sullivan Hospital System

*An enduring and powerful part of the change process at SHS was an employee-designed recognition program called "Circle of Excellence." Although similar to SHS's previous rewards programs, this program specifically targeted those behaviors identified in the firm's vision. With past programs, all nominees received an award or the nomination process was so bureaucratic, employees were discouraged from participating. The new program, however, set clear standards of expected behavior; utilized a simple, but verifiable form of peer nomination—an employee review panel to select award winners; and allowed employees to accumulate points to higher award levels for multiple winners. Further, the process and results were considered an important form of communication (according to the information plan developed earlier) that reinforced new, desired behaviors.*

---

Recognizing success also provides an important opportunity to renew commitment to a change process; hence, it should be timed appropriately. For example, if the organization's leadership believes the firm is nearing the bottom of the implementation curve (see Figure 8.1), then it is a good time to break out an award ceremony.

The ceremony will revitalize attention and commitment to the change and signal the kinds of accomplishments to be achieved.

### Making Change Stick

In the final activity associated with controlling the change process, organization leadership transfers ownership and responsibility to lower levels in the organization and makes the new behaviors a part of the fabric of the organization. Typically, after a change has been made, there is considerable variation in the execution of the new process. The first activity in making change stick is to give responsibility and authority for improving the process to the managers and organization members who own it. Such empowerment requires that the appropriate types of information, knowledge and skill, and incentives exist to support the effort (Lawler, 1986), thereby ensuring ownership of and commitment to the new processes. As a result, other people become responsible for organizational improvement and learning, thus freeing senior leadership to move on to other changes and activities. This also contributes to the second activity: teaching the new behaviors and processes to new members of the organization as the "right" way to perform. When these new behaviors become expected behaviors, an important shift in the organization's culture will have occurred.

### Summary

In this chapter and Chapter 7, we described the development and implementation of the SCP. We discussed the desired strategic orientation and the various changes, costs, and activities required to move the organization from its current strategic orientation ($S_1/O_1$) to the desired future state ($S_2/O_2$). The SCP itself is dominated by the results of a strategic change requirements analysis. This analysis allows the senior management team to build budgets, a responsibility chart, a commitment plan, and an information plan, all of which will be used to guide the strategic change implementation. The process of implementing the SCP is based on sound principles of leadership, including making the vision real, providing resources and support, and controlling the process of change.

This chapter concludes our description of how to apply the ISC process. In the final chapter, we return to the overall purpose of this book and discuss the ISC's relevance to the organization, how it confers a sustainable competitive advantage to an organization, and what some of the results are that we have seen from implementing it.

# 9

# ISC As A Competitive Advantage

One of our central beliefs behind and primary motivations for writing this book has been that organizations with an ISC capability possess an important source of competitive advantage. Most of the book, however, has focused on explaining how the ISC process can yield improvements in performance and effectiveness in the short to medium term. Although executing the process is expected to produce learning and increase a firm's capability to change, its viability as a competitive advantage has not been emphasized. In the first part of this last chapter, we directly address this issue. The criteria of sustainability described in Chapter 5—uniqueness, value, and the inability of competitors to imitate the advantage—are expanded and applied to the ISC process. Against these criteria, we conclude that a strategic change capability does represent an important opportunity for sustained competitive advantage.

In the second part of the chapter, we complete our case studies of the hospital system and the legal publishing firm by reporting on some of the results achieved through the application of the ISC process.

In the third part of this chapter, we describe the changes that many organizations will need to make to facilitate the organization's adoption of ISC and benefit from it as a competitive advantage. This discussion is motivated by our experience with organizations and the number of questions we have received from managers and OD/HR practitioners about how to install this capability in their organizations.

## How ISC Is A Sustainable Competitive Advantage

In Chapter 5, we described the necessary and sufficient conditions for dominant and distinctive competences to produce a sustainable competitive advantage. Competences had to be unique or different, valued by customers, and difficult for competitors to imitate. In this section, we elaborate on these criteria and apply them to the ISC process. This discussion is intended to answer the question, "How does a well-developed strategic change process yield a sustainable competitive advantage for the organization?"

### *Is the Capability to Manage Strategic Change Unique or Different?*

The first and most fundamental criteria of a sustainable advantage is that the resource or capability be different or unique. From our perspective, this is an interesting place to start because there is nothing unique about the basic resources of strategic change. All organizations possess, to some degree, organizational change and strategic management skills and knowledge. These skills and knowledge can reside in the human resources department (HRD), a quality department, line management, or senior management. Given the ubiquitous nature of these resources, according to the theory, there is no chance for competitive advantage. However, it is the very fact that these elemental resources of strategic change are probably found in different places in the organization and tend to operate somewhat independently that creates the opportunity for a shrewd initiative to produce a unique capability.

The uniqueness criterion really concerns *how* resources are combined, practiced, and utilized, not the uniqueness of the individual resources themselves. Different organizations within an industry may have similar amounts of cash, technological know-how, brand image, or human resources. However, they can combine them in particular ways, into routines or patterns of activities, that truly are unique. For example, Benetton, like other clothing retailers, has information systems, fashion designers, market researchers, and distribution systems. But Benetton has found a way to combine these basic skills and resources to make faster and better decisions in order to respond to markets in a more timely fashion and bring new products to market quicker.

In addition, the generally high failure rate of major strategic and organizational changes at least opens the possibility that the integration of strategic management and organizational change knowledge and skills into a routine or capability would, in fact, be a unique process. The long-term success of firms like Pepsi, General Electric, Motorola, HP, and Xerox—all of which have shown the ability to formulate and implement major strategic changes over and over again during their existence—is testament to the power of change management and to its relative scarcity. Because change and strategy skills and knowledge tend to operate independently of each other in most organizations, combining them into a single process would create an extraordinary capability for the firm in a particular industry or strategic group.

### Is ISC A Valued Capability?

The second criteria for competitive advantage is that the competence must be valued by customers or be valuable in some way. Value is typically determined by customers. If they describe the competence as desirable and are willing to pay an amount greater than its opportunity cost, it's valuable. But the ISC process has no "direct" customers. So what value does or could an ISC competence have?

On the one hand, an ISC competence is valuable because it is associated with traditional strategic planning. Strategic planning tends to be highly valued because of its close association with and emphasis on performance. However, the other parts of an ISC competence—change management skills and knowledge—are not as highly valued because they are not always closely correlated with improved performance. By itself, then, an ISC competence is not clearly and unambiguously associated with value.

On the other hand, we think ISC's value as a competence is better understood in terms of its time utility. That is, value often accrues to products, services, or activities that occur infrequently but when needed are crucial to success. When strategic change is necessary, the most valuable resource an organization can have is a change process.

Case histories of large organizations, such as GM, Kodak, and AT&T, provide ample evidence that years of managing incremental changes can produce cultures and organizations that are unable to recognize substantive environmental change and carry out the necessary strategic changes. Many organizations, when faced with the need for change and recognizing that they do not have the internal resources or processes to implement change, often turn to external consultants to import the technology. However, organizations that possess a strategic change process may have the ability to challenge the status quo *and* direct activities toward constructive change more quickly than their competitors can. Such an organization would have a clear advantage with regard to long-term survival and superior performance.

Unfortunately, traditional strategic planning processes have not been able to fill that role. In many organizations, strategic planning is as routinized as filling out an application for employment. The standardization of the process, the limited participation, the filtering of information, or the fudging of numbers to make growth seem possible for the most outdated products and services dooms the process to that of recommending incremental adjustments. When real change is necessary, the firm's senior management is isolated from the realities of the marketplace. Thus an opportunity to infuse strategic planning with the OD Perspective exists because of shortcomings in the traditional process. Strategic planning has not tended to build commitment to or ownership of a vision or desirable future and has had difficulty implementing selected strategies. As we discussed in Chapter 4, success in today's economy is more and more dependent on the execution and implementation of selected strategies. As a result, change management skills or the ability to implement strategic initiatives can grow in status if they can be integrated into strategic planning processes. Establishing such an integration, as noted earlier in the chapter, will be difficult. In the final part of this chapter, we discuss the issues associated with building up an organization's change capability.

Our tentative conclusion, therefore, is that if an organization can establish a viable strategic change process, such a process will have high value over time. Its value could be measured in terms of the relative ease with which the organization is able to initiate and implement strategic changes in comparison to its competitors. At the very least, it would be an interesting research subject.

### Can An ISC Capability Be Imitated?

The third criteria for a sustainable competitive advantage requires that the organization not only possess some unique and valuable capabilities but that the capability be difficult or impossible to imitate. If competitors can replicate the capability easily, then there is no advantage. Neither the amount of the benefit (profits or rents) nor the time the firm monopolizes the benefit will be sufficient to recoup the cost associated with developing the resource or competence. Similar to Lawler's (1992) argument that successfully implementing a high-involvement design is an advantage because it is difficult to imitate, the capability to make integrated strategic changes is quite defensible because it, too, will be most difficult to imitate.

As already mentioned, part of ISC's uniqueness is that it requires the integration of two independently operating processes:

1. The change management process
2. The strategic management process

Because these processes operate independently, integrating them will be difficult to imitate for at least two reasons. First, as earlier suggested, the traditional strategic planning process is more valued than is change management. As a result, successful integration of these two processes will not be easy. We address some of the issues in the final section.

Second, strategic management and change management operate on different assumptions. Strategy is based on economics and finance while OD is based on behavioral science and organizational theory. Designing an integrated strategic change process will be difficult. This is especially true for people who have grown up with a particular discipline's paradigm because they will not quickly see the commonalities.

Further, an ISC capability will be difficult to imitate because it is used infrequently and is relatively transparent to competitors. We believe an organization will need to make substantive changes in its strategic orientation infrequently. The environmental changes sufficient to require reorientations, for example, do not occur often (Tushman and Anderson, 1986). Any firm that is reorienting constantly is by definition in a state of chaos (Wheatley, 1993), stuck in the middle (Porter, 1980), or reacting (Miles and Snow, 1978). Such a firm is not likely to be a high performer. A much more likely scenario is where the environment has changed in minor ways, thereby prompting a firm to revise or adapt its current strategic orientation or simply to converge. The popular press and many business writers seem too sensationalist in their exhortations to organizations that they should make radical change. As a result, we believe there will be little need to apply the ISC process all the time.

In addition, because strategic change requires time, a competitor that wants to copy or imitate the process might be seeing only the strategic analysis step, the strategy making step, the VIP process, or some phase of implementation and so will not see the whole picture. This is because the strategic change capability is basically transparent, even invisible. Once an organization develops the routines associated with conducting a VIP process or visioning or designing a strategic orientation, so much of what goes on is not visible to outsiders; hence, imitating the process directly is virtually impossible. Instead, any organization that would want to imitate the process would have to innovate and adapt the process to its own situation...a costly, difficult, and time-consuming endeavor, as we've already implied.

Hence, the ISC process is difficult to imitate because it is difficult to achieve in the first place and difficult to see once it becomes a reality. As a result, competitors will be unable to know or understand why an organization was able to adapt quickly to a variety of external jolts. In addition, given the uniqueness of each firm's situation, culture, technology, and history, the likelihood that a competitor could take a particular organization's ISC process and apply it without modification is extremely low.

In sum, we believe that the ISC process can be a unique, valuable, and defensible competence. Because the key resources—strategic management and change management skills and knowledge —tend to operate independently in most organizations, integrating them into a single process represents a unique routine. The difficulty of accomplishing the integration and its transparency will make the routine defensible. Finally, we propose that the routine's value will be a function of its ability to help the organization more quickly identify the need for and to implement strategic change.

## What Are the Results from ISC?

A competitive advantage must deliver results; otherwise, by definition, it is not an advantage. The results from the two case studies described throughout this book are not a direct measure of ISC's sustainability as an advantage, but they do provide some information about its usefulness and utility.

### Legal Publishing Company/Withers-Messall

Both LPC and WM faced important and substantive changes in their environments. As a result, LPC engaged in a reorientation that altered both its strategy (entrance into the CD-ROM business) and its organization. WM, on the other hand, worked from its robust organization design and engaged in a strategy revision. In both cases, a number of external and internal events made evaluation of the strategic change process difficult. Because we used more examples of WM than LPC, we focus our attention on what happened at WM, recognizing that LPC's results and circumstance were similar.

At WM, the strategy revision called for substantial increases in CD-ROM revenues as that product line built market share. The build strategy was to be financed by a harvesting strategy in the old "print" business. In addition, the strategy was to be supported by changes to the organization's information/control systems. These quantitative and qualitative objectives were essentially met. CD-ROM revenues doubled within two years, margins in the print business increased, and the organization used its large and well-trained sales force to get closer to its customers.

What wasn't planned for were several changes in the organization itself. First, the division was part of a larger reorganization in LPC's parent company. WM ceased to report to LPC's president and instead became a subsidiary of a totally different organization. That organization had very different performance expectations. Thus many of the goals established for WM during the ISC process became somewhat irrelevant under the new firm's strategic plan. Second, the president of the division was promoted to still another division of LPC's parent. His departure was significant. He spearheaded the earlier quality effort that had produced the flexible organization. Because that effort was key to the support of the new strategy, its continued development had become his responsibility, while the other vice presidents had been left to tackle the strategic issues. When he left, there was a breach in leadership of the structure's development. Finally, the vice president of marketing and sales also left the organization. She had been a powerful influence in the development of the sales force that was widely regarded in the industry.

Thus, while many of the strategic objectives were met, there were clearly a number of other changes that prevented a clear and unambiguous assessment of ISC's success in this situation. From the participants' point of view, they had engaged in a process that had produced a clear set of action priorities that built on their organizational strengths. As a team, they had consensus about their direction and the steps it would take to reach their objectives.

### Sullivan Hospital System Results

The Sullivan Hospital System, as a result of the strategic adaptation, showed solid performance results, many of which were directly attributable to its strategic change efforts. In the paragraphs that follow, we review the results for market share, physician satisfaction, and inpatient satisfaction—three key measures of hospital performance. In addition, the average length of stay, operating margins, and overall capacity utilization measures improved, although these measures were significantly influenced by other changes at the hospital that were not a formal part of the strategic change effort.

One of the most satisfying results from the strategic change efforts at SHS was the improvement in physician satisfaction. Prior to the effort, there had been no systematic effort to understand physician needs. The first formal survey was conducted in 1992. From 1992 to 1993, overall physician satisfaction increased 22 percent at the main hospital and 2 percent at the smaller hospital. The 2-percent figure seems small only because the initial efforts and results from the Physician Quality Council meetings had produced very high satisfaction levels by the 1992 survey (77.2 percent of the physicians were satisfied or very satisfied). At the main hospital, however, the 1992 results indicated that only 66 percent of physicians were satisfied or very satisfied. By 1993, that figure had risen to 80.6 percent. The overall results were explained by the corresponding increases in physician perceptions of the quality of nursing care (19-percent increase at the main hospital); of the medical records process (16-percent increase); and of the scheduling and admissions process (12-percent increase). Each of these areas had received considerable attention from the work redesign process or from a quality improvement team.

The average overall inpatient satisfaction levels based on one hundred random phone calls each quarter during the hospitals' fiscal years are shown in Table 9.1. The worst that can be said for overall inpatient satisfaction during this time is that it stayed fairly stable for the hospital system. Between 1991 and 1994, inpatient satisfaction increased 0.7 percent at the main hospital and declined 0.2 percent at the smaller hospital. However, the main hospital showed a 7-percent increase between 1992 and 1994, and the trend appears to be holding stable in the first quarter of fiscal year 1995. Similarly, the smaller hospital's ratings have remained fairly high and consistent. It was the

**Table 9.1**
*Overall Inpatient Satisfaction Levels by Hospital by Fiscal Year*

|  | 1991 | 1992 | 1993 | 1994 | 1995 (1st Qtr) |
|---|---|---|---|---|---|
| *Main Hospital* | 84.3 | 79.5 | 83.5 | 84.9 | 85.7 |
| *Smaller Hospital* | 84.3 | 84.6 | 84.5 | 84.1 | 90.0 |

first hospital in the system to ever break the 90-percent mark, which it did in the first quarter of fiscal year 1995.

Finally, between 1989 and 1993, SHS's market share declined 7.14 percent. It posted annual market share declines of 3.5 percent from 1989 to 1990 and 10.43 percent from 1990 to 1991. However, the ISC process was initiated in January 1990, and the trend since has been encouraging. SHS *increased* its market share 0.3 percent from 1991 to 1992 and showed a 7.14-percent increase in market share from 1992 to 1993. The first two quarters of 1994 continued this positive trend, showing market share increases over the first two quarters of 1993. Hospital administrators attribute most of the increase to the Physician Quality Council efforts that directly targeted physician satisfaction.

## Developing An Integrated Strategic Change Capability

Integrated strategic change infuses strategic management principles with the OD Perspective—forming a process that helps organizations and their members decide when and how to change their strategic orientations. As we have defined it, this is neither a frequent nor a minor occurrence. While the pace of change is increasing and will call on organizations to make these fundamental changes more often, the organization will not make these changes every year. Instead, important external and internal changes will occur infrequently, requiring a major organizational response. Our belief is that the organization must have the capability to recognize when fundamental strategic change is necessary, and possess the skills, knowledge, and processes to carry it out.

Unfortunately, while most organizations possess skills and knowledge in both strategic management and change management, the former are more prevalent and more valued than the latter. This is also unfortunate because successful strategic change processes may be more dependent on the OD Perspective than on strategic management skills and knowledge. In the following sections, we explain

1. why most organizations either do not or cannot initiate and implement strategic change, and
2. how they can build up their change management competences.

### Mainlining the OD Perspective

We have found it helpful to array the four steps of ISC in a matrix (Figure 9.1). It suggests that ISC process is concerned with two issues.

1. The *content* versus the *process* of strategic management.
2. The *what* versus the *how* of strategic orientation.

*Content* refers to the body of knowledge that contributes to strategy and organization design, such as economics, finance, or organizational theory. *Process* refers to the method in which the content is applied, determined, or understood. The second issue concerns the development of a strategic orientation. The *what* comprises the specific elements of strategic orientation versus *how* strategic orientation will change from its present state to its desired future state. Strategic analysis, for example, is primarily a diagnostic process that attempts to determine what the organization's current strategic orientation is. Strategy making is concerned with what the future strategic orientation is going to be, but is much more content driven than is strategic analysis.

Thus, in the top row of Figure 9.1 are the first two steps in ISC —both process and content steps. However, they are primarily concerned with the elements of strategic orientation. In the bottom row, the concern is how the strategic orientation will change. It deals with the strategic change plan. In SCP design, we are involved with determining the content of the SCP and how the strategic orientation will change. Finally, in SCP implementation, the concern is the process of how the changes are actually made.

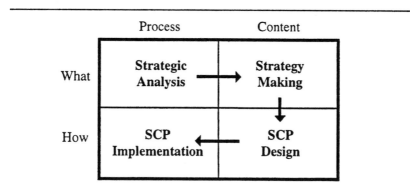

**Figure 9.1**
*How the OD Perspective Influences Strategic Change*

Examining this matrix reveals how important the OD Perspective is to the strategic change process. In three of the four cells of the matrix, change management skills and knowledge are required. The OD Perspective is especially well suited to assist in the design of diagnostic processes (strategic analysis), the construction of strategic change plans, and the implementation of strategic change plans. While strategic content issues are important, it is strategic processes and the *how* of change that determine whether or not a good strategy is well implemented.

Successful strategic change therefore requires nothing less than placing the OD Perspective into the mainstream of organizational thinking. Given strategic management's relatively high presence and value in an organization, if a firm wishes to develop an ISC capability, the key development activity should be to build up the organization's change management competences. The question here is, "How?" Many forward thinking organizations, such as PepsiCo, Arco Transportation Company, Intel, and AT&T, have begun to formulate a response. These organizations have begun to radically alter the traditional mission and activities of their human resources function. Although an organization can build and acquire change management skills in any part of the organization, the one place where it makes the most sense to attain these skills is the human resource development (HRD) department.

### Building Change Competences

In order for ISC to become a viable competitive advantage, most organizations need to develop a relevant and powerful change management competence that can be integrated with traditional strategic management processes. The emphasis on speed, quality, and productivity in response to global competition, technological change, innovations in work design, and social trends has heightened firms' awareness of the need for these skills. At all levels, firms are becoming considerably more knowledgeable and more attuned to the contribution the HRD function can make. As the ability to create, manage, and respond to change has become increasingly important, organizations are becoming more aware that they are not very skillful in these areas. They are looking for leadership and expertise to help them.

In response to questions from human resource and organization development professionals, who want to begin to establish greater change competences in their organizations, we have compiled an organization "to do" list. It outlines the changes and activities that we believe organizations need to implement in order to build an ISC capability into their organizations. Since the HRD function is the most likely to contain the nucleus of these competences, most of the changes are aimed there. The changes include the following methods for building a change management competence:

1. Focus HRD's mission on alignment
2. Drive the strategic management process
3. Generalize, downsize, and outsource
4. Emphasize strategic training and development
5. Align appraisal and rewards with strategies

*Focus HRD's Mission on Alignment.* The business of a strategically focused HRD function should be driving organizational change—bringing the elements of a firm's strategic orientation into tighter and tighter alignment with each other. HRD must build itself into a relevant center of change management. It must develop dominant and distinctive competences of change management and implementation. This will serve to signal that the department is primarily concerned with how to assist the organization in developing strategies, structures, and processes that support each other.

However, there is a second aspect to alignment. In addition to driving organizational changes and bringing the elements of the firm's strategic orientation into better alignment, change management competences should also be focused on three activities.

1. Understanding the organization's alignment with its environment.
2. Monitoring changes in the environment.
3. Driving decisions about when it is appropriate to engage in an integrated strategic change process.

These activities involve

- collecting performance, productivity, and other effectiveness data,
- comparing performance against goals,
- collecting data from throughout the organization on competitor moves and signals, new technologies, supplier changes, customer wants and needs, and so on, and

- circulating this information throughout the organization frequently so the organization is less likely to be surprised, and more likely to be aware when change is necessary.

By reorienting the mission of one department toward alignment issues, the organization is better positioned to increase its change management competences, improve the efficiency of its information and control systems, and increase the chances of not being caught off guard.

*Drive the Strategic Management Process.* A second method for building a change management competence is to put the HRD function in charge of strategic planning. The human resource and OD executives are too often missing from the one place where their capabilities can have the most impact on and value to their organization—the strategic management process. For historic, and now obsolete reasons, most CEOs and traditional line executives viewed strategic planning as the *hard* side of business dominated by analysis, quantification, and ruthless strategizing. These were areas where the *soft* HRD and OD skills were unnecessary. Perhaps as a remnant of this outdated approach, the HRD function has not been among the important influencers or implementers in the strategic change efforts we have discussed. It typically lacks the *horsepower* to drive the strategic change process. However, we do believe that HRD professionals can and should play a central role in managing strategic change.

Two steps must be taken in order for HRD professionals to become a driver of the process:

1. To reorient their mission towards alignment and lobby to be placed in charge of the process, and
2. To learn the tools, techniques, and logic of strategy.

Reorienting HRD's mission towards alignment is not sufficient to drive the strategic planning process. Human resource/OD executives need to lobby to be placed in charge of the process. This is likely to entail some risk. For example, driving the process may require a structural change like placing the strategic planning staff in the HRD function. Since strategic management competences are typically more valued than change management competences, strategic planning personnel may see this as a demotion. However, such a move is preferable to placing the HRD staff under strategic planning's organization. In that position, HRD's traditional low-power status prevents it from having an equal say. Having strategic-planning expertise in the HRD function allows for a greater likelihood of cross-pollination of ideas and a greater chance that the two functions will act as equals in the process.

Better yet, the strategic planning function might be abolished altogether. If projections about the increasing pace of change, the more educated workforce, and the value of empowering people with value-added decisions are true, then strategic thinking should replace strategic planning. This move requires an HRD strategy that seeks to build strategic capabilities into the line organization itself (see the training and development section below). Eliminating the strategic planning function altogether should cause the line organization to be more dependent on leadership and expertise in a strategic- and alignment-oriented HRD function. In this role, the HRD/OD function can help to shape and drive strategy within the organization. Strategy will be owned by the line organization and will seek assistance in getting strategies implemented.

For HRD personnel to become credible drivers of the strategic planning process, they must learn, understand, and speak the language of strategy. This means becoming comfortable with concepts of finance, accounting, economics, and marketing. By combining the hard and soft sides of business, HR/OD professionals will have gained an important glimpse of the big picture they are trying to influence. Similarly, they must educate strategic planners on the value and relevance of including soft issues in the strategic management process.

***Generalize, Downsize, and Outsource.*** The third method for building a change management competence is to focus the HRD function on value-added change activities and away from "administrivia." In our vision, HRD is much smaller in terms of the number of people employed, but much more knowledgeable and skilled in a broad range of topics. The HRD function must be staffed with people who possess both strategic management and change management competences as well as the traditional knowledge of human resource management. The HRD generalist, who is versed in all of these areas, is primarily a change consultant to line management. In essence, HRD becomes a group of strategy formulation and implementation consultants—measured by its reputation among line managers. That reputation is based on its abilities

- to help the line organization formulate winning strategies,
- to improve the effectiveness and efficiency of core, value-added processes,

- to align elements of the organization's strategic orientation, and
- to prepare the organization for change in the future.

In fact, we believe that the HRD function should become accountable for this responsibility as well. This can be done by tying the HRD generalist's compensation directly to the line manager's budget. If the HRD function is ineffective or irrelevant, the "market" will signal this and its staff will be out of a job.

This new emphasis on alignment and driving the strategic planning process implies that many of the traditional HRD functions, such as compensation, benefits, hiring, outplacement, and so on need to be realigned. Recent trends toward network organizations and virtual corporations, accelerated by reengineering and "right-sizing," have pointed out that growth hides waste. Many organizations carry out work and manage processes that do not make a direct, value-added contribution to the organization's goals and objectives. The result has been the elimination of work, levels, and whole processes, many of which are outsourced to vendors that specialize in particular functions. We suspect that human resources, driven by an administrative mission left over from their days as the "personnel department" and by increasing legal and regulatory constraints, also carries too much overhead.

Forward-thinking organizations are moving away from administratively-driven HRD functions and reengineering themselves. These firms are taking advantage of vendors dedicated to compensation administration, benefits administration, standard training and development, and other routine program administration duties. For example, several organizations have implemented touch sensitive computer screens to administer benefits programs such as health care and tuition reimbursement. This frees up the HRD staff to focus on direct, value-added activities to support the line organization.

*Emphasize Strategic Training and Development.* The fourth method for building a change management competence is the most direct. Not all training and development activities need to be or should be outsourced to vendors. The direct development of strategic change management competences within the organization should remain a responsibility of the HRD function while more traditional subjects such as communications skills, basic technical training, statistical process control, problem-solving, project management, and so on can be contracted. In addition, change management skills and knowledge should be taught alongside strategic management skills and knowledge. Change management topics should focus on diagnostic, intervention design, visioning, building consensus, action planning, conflict management, and similar skills. Strategic management should focus on the need to understand basic strategies, organization design options, the design of information/control systems, and competitor analysis.

While these subjects are offered by many training firms, we believe that they can and should be tailored to the organization's particular strategies and objectives. This tailoring process should be conducted by the organization's HRD staff who are already educated in these areas. Training and developing in areas specific to the organization's needs permits focused development efforts and results in quicker implementation of chosen strategies, improved alignments, and the building of competences for the future.

*Align Appraisal and Rewards with Strategies.* The final method for building change management competences into the organization is to align appraisal and reward systems with business strategies, goal achievement, and strategic human resource development. An increasing number of consultants and authors are calling for strategic human resource management. In this line of thinking, the traditional selection, training, appraisal, and reward system functions are tied more closely with the firm's strategy. This fits perfectly with our belief that the mission of the HRD function should be associated with alignment. The required skills, knowledge, and competences required of organizational members to meet both long and short range strategic objectives should be planned. Some activities that should be the HRD organization's high priorities are

- fitting appraisal processes to work designs,
- paying for performance, and
- building skills and knowledge in key competence areas.

As noted, the HRD organization itself may not perform all these functions. In line with the downsize and outsource initiative, many of these activities can be performed by outside vendors. That does not mean that the HRD function is not responsible for aligning these activities together and with other strategic orientation elements.

The reward system, an important part of any HRD organization, has for too long been an administrative function and not strategically leveraged. In the new HRD department, the power associated with reward system design and implementation should be captured. The reward system represents a key method for aligning strategy and organization design to the behaviors of people. The use of compensation innovations such as gainsharing, skill-based pay, employee stock ownership, and pay for performance is spreading. However, it is not common practice and represents an important, but underutilized, weapon in aligning strategic orientations. The organization will increase its alignment and be more prepared for change in the future by rewarding and recognizing strategic thinking, the accomplishment of strategic objectives, and the acquisition of strategic change skills and knowledge.

Building a change competence in the organization is the single most important activity a firm can pursue if it wants to reap the advantages of integrated strategic change as a competitive advantage. Many organizations, buffeted by global, technological, and social change, are beginning to alter their views of the HRD function. This reorientation of views is being backed up by affirmative actions that give HRD a central and driving role in the formulation and implementation of strategic change. However, too many organizations have not initiated this effort. As we described it, many organizations will have a difficult time making these changes. They may see them as strategically irrelevant, too costly, or too time consuming. This is precisely why the initiative should be taken immediately and why making these changes can result in a sustainable advantage.

## Summary

In this chapter, we have defended the idea that an ISC process can be a source of long-term competitive advantage and demonstrated that its application can affect firm performance. We also proposed some changes to the traditional HRD function that will go a long way toward helping to implement ISC as a core, albeit latent, organizational process.

The central focus of this book has been that strategy and organization development can and should be integrated. By infusing strategic planning processes with the OD Perspective, organizations can understand better when and how to make substantive changes in their strategic orientations. Without this integration, we fear organizations will continue to generate elegant strategies that fail to get implemented or effectively implement organizational changes that have but a tenuous relationship to firm performance. We hope we have provided a means for thinking about this integration, demonstrated its application, and encouraged OD practitioners and line managers alike to attempt strategic changes that both increase performance and maximize human potential.

# References

Argyris, C. 1970. *Intervention Theory and Method.* Reading, MA: Addison-Wesley.

Barney, J. and W. Ouchi (Eds.). 1986. *Organization Economics.* San Francisco: Jossey-Bass.

Beckhard, R. 1969. *Organization Development.* Reading, MA: Addison-Wesley.

Beckhard, R. and R. Harris. 1987. *Organization Transitions.* Reading, MA: Addison-Wesley.

Beckhard, R. and W. Pritchard. 1992. *Changing the Essence.* San Francisco: Jossey-Bass.

Bennis, W. and B. Nanus. 1985. *Leaders.* New York: Harper and Row.

Block, P. 1993. *Stewardship.* San Francisco: Berrett-Koehler.

Bonoma, T.V. 1985. *The Marketing Edge: Making Strategies Work.* New York: The Free Press.

Burke, W. 1992. *Organization Development: A Normative View.* Reading, MA: Addison-Wesley.

Buller, P. 1988. "For successful strategic change: Blend OD practices with strategic management," *Organization Dynamics* (Winter) 42–55.

Cummings, T. G. and C. G. Worley. 1992. *Organization Development and Change* (Fifth Edition). St. Paul, MN: West Publishing.

Drucker, P. 1974. *Management: Tasks, Responsibilities, Practices.* New York: Harper and Row.

Fombrun, C. 1992. *Turning Points.* New York: McGraw-Hill.

Fombrun, C. and A. Ginsberg. 1990. "Shifting gears: Enabling change in corporate aggressiveness," *Strategic Management Journal,* 11 (1990) 297–308.

Galbraith J. and R. Kazanjian. 1986. *Strategy Implementation: Structure, Systems and Process* (Second edition). St. Paul, MN: West Publishing.

Ginsberg, A. 1988. "Measuring and modeling changes in strategy: Theoretical foundations and empirical directions," *Strategic Management Journal,* 9, 559–575.

Ginsberg, A. and J. Grant. 1985. "Research on strategic change: Theoretical and methodological issues," *Academy of Management Proceedings,* 45th meeting of the Academy of Management, Boston, MA.

Grant, R. 1992. *Contemporary Strategy Analysis.* Cambridge, MA: Basil Blackwell.

Greiner, L. 1972. "Evolution and revolution as organizations grow," *Harvard Business Review,* 50(4):37–46.

Greiner, L. 1986. "Top management politics and organizational change," In S. Srivastva et al. (Editors.), *Executive Power,* San Francisco: Jossey-Bass.

Greiner, L. and A. Bhambri. 1989. "New CEO intervention and the dynamics of deliberate strategic change." *Strategic Management Journal,* 10 (Summer) 67–86.

Hambrick, D. 1981. "Environment, strategy, and power within top management teams," *Strategic Management Journal,* 26:253–276.

Hammer, M. and J. Champy. 1992. *Re-engineering the Corporation.* New York: Harper and Row.

Hart, S. "An integrative framework for strategy-making processes," *Academy of Management Review,* 17(2):327–351.

Hayes, R. and W. Abernathy. 1980. "Managing our way to economic decline," *Harvard Business Review* (July–August) 67–77.

Hofer, C. and D. Schendel. 1978. *Strategy Formulation.* St. Paul, MN: West Publishing.

Hrebiniak, L. and W. Joyce. 1984. *Implementing Strategy.* New York· Macmillan Publishing.

Huber, G., K. Sutcliffe, C. Miller, and W. Glick. 1991. "Understanding and predicting organizational change," paper presented at the National Academy of Management, Miami, FL.

Jamieson, D. and J. O'Mara. 1991. *Managing Workforce 2000.* San Francisco: Jossey-Bass.

Jelinek, M. and J. Litterer. "Why OD must become strategic," in *Research in Organization Change and Development,* Vol. 2, Ed. W. Pasmore and R. Woodman. Greenwich, CT: JAI Press.

Lawler, E. 1986. *High-Involvement Management.* San Francisco: Jossey-Bass.

Lawler, E. 1992. *The Ultimate Advantage.* San Francisco: Jossey-Bass.

Lippitt, R., J. Watson and B. Westley. 1958. *The Dynamics of Planned Change.* New York: Harcourt, Brace and World.

R. Lurie, B. Huston, and D. Yoffie. 1989. *Intel Corporation, 1988.* HBS Case 9-389-063. Boston: Harvard Business School.

McKelvey, B. 1982. *Organizational Systematics: Taxonomy, Evolution, Classification.* Los Angeles: University of California Press.

Miller, D. and P. Friesen. 1980. "Momentum and revolution in organizational adaptation." *Academy of Management Journal,* 23(4): 591–614.

Miles, R. and C. Snow. 1978. *Organization Strategy, Structure and Process.* New York: McGraw-Hill.

Mintzberg, H. 1994. *The Rise and Fall of Strategic Planning.* Boston: Harvard Business School Press.

Mintzberg, H. and F. Westley. "Cycles of organizational change," *Strategic Management Journal,* 13 (Special Issue) 39–60.

Mumford, E. and A. Pettigrew. 1975. *Implementing Strategic Decisions.* London: Longman.

Nadler, D. and M. Tushman. 1992. "Designing organizations that have good fit: A framework for understanding new architectures," in D. Nadler, M. Gerstein, R. Shaw and Associates (Eds.), *Organizational Architecture.* San Francisco: Jossey-Bass.

Peteraf, M. 1993. "The cornerstones of competitive advantage: A resource-based view," *Strategic Management Journal,* 14(3):179–192.

Pettigrew, A. 1985. *The Awakening Giant.* Cambridge: Basil Blackwell.

Pettigrew, A. 1992. "The character and significance of strategy process research," *Strategic Management Journal,* 13 (Special Issue): 5–16.

Porter, M. 1980. *Competitive Strategy.* New York: Free Press.

Porter, M. 1985. *Competitive Advantage.* New York: Free Press.

Porter, M. 1987. "From competitive advantage to corporate strategy," *Harvard Business Review* (May–June) 43–59.

Porter, M. 1991. "Towards a dynamic theory of strategy," *Strategic Management Journal,* 12 (Special Issue): 95–117.

Prahalad, C. and G. Hamel. 1990. "The core competence of the corporation," *Harvard Business Review* (May–June): 79–91.

Robert, M. 1993. *Strategy Pure and Simple.* New York: McGraw-Hill.

Rumelt, R. 1974. *Strategy, Structure and Economic Performance.* Boston: Harvard University Press.

Rumelt, R., D. Schendel, and D. Teece. 1991. "Strategic management and economics," *Strategic Management Journal,* 12:5–29.

Schein, E. 1993. *Organization Culture and Leadership.* San Francisco: Jossey-Bass.

Senge, P. 1990. *The Fifth Discipline: The Art and Practice of the Learning Organization.* New York: Doubleday.

Sherman, S. 1993. "The new computer revolution," *Fortune,* 127:56–80.

Snow, C. and D. Hambrick. 1980. "Measuring organizational strategies: Some theoretical and methodological problems," *Academy of Management Review,* 5:527–538.

Tichy, N. 1983. *Managing Strategic Change.* New York: Wiley and Sons.

Tichy, N. and S. Sherman. 1993. *Control Your Destiny or Someone Else Will.* New York: Doubleday.

Tushman, M. and E. Romanelli. 1985. "Organizational evolution: A metamorphosis model of convergence and reorientation," in L. L. Cummings and Barry Staw (Editors), *Research in Organization Behavior,* Vol. 7. Greenwich, CT: JAI Press.

Tushman, M. and P. Anderson. 1986. "Technological discontinuities and organizational environments," *Administrative Science Quarterly,* 31:439–465.

Wheatley, M. 1992. *Leadership and the New Science.* San Francisco: Berrett-Koehler.

Weisbord, M. 1976. "Organization diagnosis: Six places to look for trouble with or without a theory," *Group and Organization Studies* (December): 430–447.

Weisbord, M. 1991. *Productive Workplaces.* San Francisco: Jossey-Bass.

Worley, C. 1991. "The dynamics of strategic change: Unraveling the impacts of technology, management and prior performance," Unpublished doctoral dissertation, University of Southern California, Los Angeles, CA.